Maker Innovations Series

Jump start your path to discovery with the Apress Maker Innovations series! From the basics of electricity and components through to the most advanced options in robotics and Machine Learning, you'll forge a path to building ingenious hardware and controlling it with cutting-edge software. All while gaining new skills and experience with common toolsets you can take to new projects or even into a whole new career.

The Apress Maker Innovations series offers projects-based learning, while keeping theory and best processes front and center. So you get hands-on experience while also learning the terms of the trade and how entrepreneurs, inventors, and engineers think through creating and executing hardware projects. You can learn to design circuits, program AI, create IoT systems for your home or even city, and so much more!

Whether you're a beginning hobbyist or a seasoned entrepreneur working out of your basement or garage, you'll scale up your skillset to become a hardware design and engineering pro. And often using low-cost and open-source software such as the Raspberry Pi, Arduino, PIC microcontroller, and Robot Operating System (ROS). Programmers and software engineers have great opportunities to learn, too, as many projects and control environments are based in popular languages and operating systems, such as Python and Linux.

If you want to build a robot, set up a smart home, tackle assembling a weather-ready meteorology system, or create a brand-new circuit using breadboards and circuit design software, this series has all that and more! Written by creative and seasoned Makers, every book in the series tackles both tested and leading-edge approaches and technologies for bringing your visions and projects to life.

More information about this series at https://link.springer.com/ bookseries/17311

Learn Engineering with LEGO

A Practical Introduction to Engineering Concepts

Grady Koch

Apress®

Learn Engineering with LEGO: A Practical Introduction to Engineering Concepts

Grady Koch
Yorktown, VA, USA

ISBN-13 (pbk): 978-1-4842-9282-2   ISBN-13 (electronic): 978-1-4842-9280-8
https://doi.org/10.1007/978-1-4842-9280-8

Managing Director, Apress Media LLC: Welmoed Spahr
Acquisitions Editor: Susan McDermott
Development Editor: James Markham
Coordinating Editor: Jessica Vakili

Distributed to the book trade worldwide by Springer Science+Business Media New York, 233 Spring Street, 6th Floor, New York, NY 10013. Phone 1-800-SPRINGER, fax (201) 348-4505, e-mail orders-ny@springer-sbm.com, or visit www.springeronline.com. Apress Media, LLC is a California LLC and the sole member (owner) is Springer Science + Business Media Finance Inc (SSBM Finance Inc). SSBM Finance Inc is a **Delaware** corporation.

For information on translations, please e-mail booktranslations@springernature.com; for reprint, paperback, or audio rights, please e-mail bookpermissions@springernature.com.

Apress titles may be purchased in bulk for academic, corporate, or promotional use. eBook versions and licenses are also available for most titles. For more information, reference our Print and eBook Bulk Sales web page at http://www.apress.com/bulk-sales.

Any source code or other supplementary material referenced by the author in this book is available to readers on the Github repository: https://github.com/Apress/Learn-Engineering-with-LEGO. For more detailed information, please visit http://www.apress.com/source-code.

Printed on acid-free paper

Table of Contents

About the Author

**Grady Koch** is the author of several books about LEGO and the founder of the website hightechlego.com. He has a Ph.D. in Electrical Engineering and 35 years of experience as a research engineer at NASA Langley Research Center, where he has built optical and laser instruments that have been flown on aircraft and orbited the Earth. He has three patents in the field of lidar for studying the atmosphere and is the author or contributor of over 200 journal and conference publications. Throughout his career, Dr. Koch has mentored many interns and found that students sometimes need a little help in making the transition of what they've learned in classroom to real-world practice. These ideas of applying knowledge to practice are incorporated into his LEGO books.

About the Technical Reviewer

Vishnu Agarwal has more than seven years of experience in the field of LEGO robotics. He is the founder of ROBO-G, a robotics and STEAM education service provider. He is also the "Mentor of Change" for Atal Tinkering Lab at the Vidyashilp Academy. Vishnu has successfully coached teams in the World Robot Olympiad and First LEGO League competitions. Many students and teachers alike have learned STEAM concepts using LEGO education from Vishnu's courses and coaching. And he has presented a research paper on Teaching Programming and Computational Thinking to Elementary Level Children Using Lego Robotics Education Kit at T4E at IIT, Bombay.

Acknowledgments

My continued appreciation goes out to the LEGO Group for their phenomenal building toy. To me, LEGO is much more than a toy. LEGO can be used and enjoyed on many levels for many uses. Sure, it's a toy, and a rather engaging one that attracts and brings together people of all ages. But LEGO is also an excellent tool to teach science and engineering concepts, which I've used with my own kids and is a motivation for this book. Another motivation for this book is to show LEGO as a tool for invention.

To convey the concepts and inventions in this book, I've included step-by-step instructions for building exercises and projects. I made the building instructions with a combination of BrickLink Studio (bricklink. com) and LDraw (ldraw.org). BrickLink Studio is a computer-aided design (CAD) utility for building with virtual LEGO that evolved from Digital Designer developed by the LEGO Group. LDraw, originally built by James Jessiman, is another LEGO CAD package that has been expanded on by many dedicated people. There are several interfaces to the LDraw foundation. Among these interfaces, I used MLCAD (mlcad.lm-software. com) developed by Michael Lachmann, and LDCad (melkert.net/LDCAD) developed by Roland Melkert. To create building instructions from CAD models, I used the LIC utility (bugeyedmonkeys.com) developed by Remi Gagne and LPub3D (sourceforge.net/projects/lpub3d) based on the work of Trevor Sandy, Kevin Clague, Leonardo Zide, Travis Cobbs, and Peter Bartfai.

ACKNOWLEDGMENTS

My appreciation is extended to Apress, whose books I've been enjoying for many years. So it's been a thrill to write for such a great publishing company for a third LEGO book. My thanks are given to Jessica Vakili and James Markham, who did fantastic work in editing. Part of writing a good book is to have an insightful technical reviewer, and Vishnu Agarwal came through in this regard.

Finally, let me thank Melissa, Kirsten, and Elias for supporting my indulgences in LEGO and building strange devices. LEGO is stuffed and scattered throughout our home, for which I apologize and promise to clean up one day.

Introduction

This book explores engineering concepts by building examples with LEGO. Fundamental principles are presented of how machines work and why they are built the way they are. There are two reasons why it may be interesting to learn these engineering concepts. The first reason is for the simple joy of tinkering with machinery. It can be a captivating experience to contemplate the inner workings of a machine that can be held in the hand to take apart, modify, and reassemble. LEGO makes such tinkering easy and, nowadays, sophisticated with the interplay of mechanical, electronic, and computer aspects found in MINDSTORMS Robot Inventor or SPIKE Prime.

The second reason is that the basic designs explored in this book can serve as a basis for customized inventions. One of the exercises or projects may provide an idea for a new project or solve a particular design challenge for a device. For example, examples are included for two fundamental drivetrains for a robot or vehicle: tank drive and rear-wheel drive. Building these two fundamental approaches provides the experience to decide on which is better suited to a customized project. Drivetrains are just one example of basic designs covered in this book. Building exercises are also laid out to build structures, gear systems, sensors, computer control, and mechanisms to spin, push, point, and shoot.

All of the parts used in the exercises and projects of this book are in the MINDSTORMS Robot Inventor set, also referred to by the part number 51515. With this set, there's no need to buy any other parts. The electronic controller, called the Hub, for Robot Inventor is programmed by connecting to a host computer or smart device that the user provides,

---

The original version of this book was revised. A correction to this book is available at https://doi.org/10.1007/978-1-4842-9280-8_10

from which an app is run to control and program inventions. The Robot Inventor app works on a wide variety of computers and smart devices including iOS, macOS, Fire OS, Windows, and Android devices. Once the app is installed on a computer or smart device, the code described in this book can be entered for each particular exercise or project. Code is also available for download on GitHub.

Most of the projects in this book make use of the Hub, which is programmed to control inventions. No prior experience is assumed in this book with programming, with a step-by-step explanation given of how computer programs are implemented from initial concept to code. Two programming languages are used, Word Blocks and Python, to work with the Hub; there is the option of using whichever language is of interest. Beginners, persons of more casual interest, or users of a smart device without a keyboard may prefer the Word Blocks version of the programs. But readers interested in advanced programming may find Python of greater interest. Many users, especially kids, start learning how to write programs with Scratch, which is quite similar to MINDSTORMS Word Blocks, and so it should be a quick adaptation to use the programs in this book. But many kids of middle-school age want to learn Python, but have a hard time. So another reason programs in this book are in both languages is to help the transition from Scratch to Python.

LEGO makes a product called SPIKE Prime as part of its Education product line primarily meant for use in schools that is a sort of cousin to Robot Inventor. The programs in this book will work in SPIKE Prime with no modification needed. Many parts are the same between SPIKE Prime and Robot Inventor, with just a difference in color. However, some of the more specialized parts are included in one set but not the other. So an owner of SPIKE Prime set will have most, but not all, of the parts used in this book. The few extra parts needed can be found individually on aftermarket parts dealers such as bricklink.com. All of the parts used in each exercise and project are described by part number in the Appendix, in case a particular part is needed.

This book explores the three specialties of software (Chapters 1 and 2), mechanical (Chapters 3–5), and electrical (Chapters 6–9) engineering. The electrical engineering chapters also incorporate the software and mechanical aspects of the earlier chapters. Each chapter has quick building exercises plus a larger concluding project. Topics in each chapter are described here in brief.

Chapter 1, "The Hub," describes working with the Hub, the device that controls motors and sensors. Instructions are given on how to power the Hub and navigate its front panel controls. The Hub can be used as a stand-alone controller, without the need to get into programming, to spin a motor, and then use a Distance Sensor to control the speed of the motor.

Chapter 2, "Programming," advances to the next level of using the Hub by programming it from the Robot Inventor app. The design of a program is described as starting from a problem statement to developing an algorithm. Implementation of an algorithm with a flowchart makes the final step of coding easier to understand. There are two options for the coding language, Word Blocks and Python, both of which are presented. Building projects include controlling the displays of the Hub, followed by a miniature dance floor decorated with light and sound effects.

Chapter 3, "Building Elements," starts an exploration of mechanical engineering concepts by touring the many parts in the Robot Inventor set used to build structures and machines. The basic structural element is the liftarm, with connections made by pins, axles, and connectors. Liftarms come in a variety of shapes, and the reasoning behind these shapes will become apparent with building exercises. These building exercises include topics in strong structures, symmetry, and linkages.

Chapter 4, "Gears," unlocks the principles of using gears to change the speed, torque, and direction from a rotational power source, like a motor. Speed and torque are critical parameters in designing robots and vehicles, and the relationship between speed and torque is explored. Moreover, building exercises show how to manipulate gear configurations to get the desired speed and torque. The concluding project of the chapter builds a two-speed transmission.

Chapter 5, "Mechanisms," explores fundamental machines for taking action to lift, spin, push, nudge, drive, or shoot. Building exercises include the example mechanisms of a ratchet, cam, differential, turntable, and dart shooter. The final chapter project combines several mechanisms to build a steerable cannon.

Chapter 6, "Motors," begins topics in electrical engineering with learning how to use motors, including programming to set speed or go to a specific angle. Practical limitations of torque and stall on motor performance are explored. Motors are integral in providing motion to robots and vehicles, and so two fundamental ways of providing steerable motion of tank drive and rear-wheel drive are presented in building examples.

Chapter 7, "The Motion Sensor," works with the sensor built into the Hub to measure tilt and orientation. The meaning of yaw, pitch, and roll is explored by building a motion alarm. Another exercise experiments with orientation of the Hub to trigger different sounds. The chapter project combines the Motion Sensor with a motor to build a machine that always points toward the ceiling, no matter the roll angle.

Chapter 8, "The Distance Sensor," incorporates distance measurement into inventions. The first exercise is to build a handheld tool to replace an old-fashioned tape measure. This sensor can also detect when an object comes close, which is put into use to modify the cannon in Chapter 5 to automatically detect and fire upon a target.

Chapter 9, "The Color Sensor," adds the capability to work with light, measuring the brightness of light and the color of objects. Building experience starts with a beeping tone generator that changes pitch depending on brightness of light. The concluding project combines ideas from earlier chapters in the book to combine the Color Sensor, motors, a linkage, and structures to sort liftarms by color.

CHAPTER 1

The Hub

The Hub, pictured in Figure 1-1, is a small computer that powers
and controls inventions. This book will show how to combine it with
sensors and motors to explore many engineering concepts. This chapter
introduces the Hub, including how to power it up, charge it, and navigate
the controls on its front panel.

While the Hub is meant to be programmed, as will be done throughout
this book, it can also control sensor- and motor-based projects by using
the front panel of the Hub alone, without any programming needed. This
chapter includes two such projects that spin a motor at various speeds.

Assembling and Charging the Hub

The Hub comes in the Robot Inventor (and SPIKE Prime) set in two
pieces: the hub and a battery, as pictured in Figure 1-2. The battery snaps
into the Hub, with little need to ever remove the battery, except perhaps
for swapping out batteries if a spare is urgently needed. The battery is
rechargeable and likely needs a fresh charging when first used. Charging
is done by the USB cable that comes in the set, with the small connector
(called a USB Mini) plugging into the Hub and the large connector (called
a USB A) plugging into a computer or USB charger. These USB connections
are shown in Figure 1-3. If plugged into a computer for charging, the Hub
powers on with a musical chirp and the front panel lights up, and the host

© Grady Koch 2023
G. Koch, *Learn Engineering with LEGO*, Maker Innovations Series,
https://doi.org/10.1007/978-1-4842-9280-8_1

computer sounds a notice that it has found new hardware—this can be ignored for now. The Hub can take a few hours for a full charge. There's a way to check for the level of battery charge, which will be described in Chapter 2. While charging, the features of the Hub can be explored as described as follows.

Figure 1-1. *The Hub is a small computer for controlling sensors and motors*

Figure 1-2. *The Hub is powered by a removable battery*

Figure 1-3. *The Hub battery is charged by a USB connection*

Controls and Displays

The Hub has several buttons, displays, and a speaker built into it that serve
to turn on the Hub and control various features. These control features on
the Hub can be for either input or output. Input functions are the buttons
on the front panel, while output functions are displays and a speaker.

There are four buttons on the front panel of the Hub used to control
functions, pictured in Figure 1-4. The center button is the power control,
which, when pressed, turns on the Hub. Another press and hold of at least
three seconds turns off the Hub. The center button also executes a program
that has been loaded into memory, as will be described in Chapter 2. Next
to the center button are the left and right buttons, used to scroll through
programs that are stored in the Hub's memory. With no programs loaded

into the Hub, these buttons don't show any effect yet. But the left and right buttons also serve to increment motor settings, as will be used later in this chapter. Another button is the Bluetooth button, which is pressed to set up a Bluetooth link. *Bluetooth* is a type of radio link between computers.

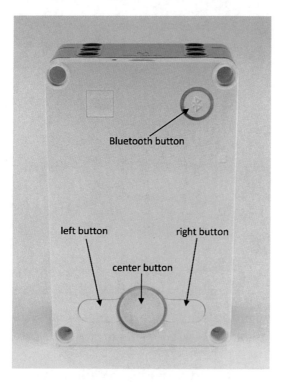

Figure 1-4. *The four input buttons on the Hub*

Two displays are part of the Hub, pictured in Figure 1-5. One display is a 5 × 5 matrix of yellow LEDs, which are used in Chapter 2 to make shapes, numbers, or letters. But this matrix display is also involved in indicating the status of the Hub. For example, after powering up the Hub, a play symbol (a triangle like on an old-fashioned tape recorder) lights up on the matrix display to indicate that things are working OK. The brightness of the 5 × 5 LED matrix can be changed, but its color can only be yellow.

Figure 1-5. *Two outputs on the front panel of the Hub are a 5 × 5 LED matrix of yellow lights and a ring around the center button*

The other display on the Hub is a colored ring around the center button. When the Hub is first powered, this ring is a white color. In Chapter 2, options will be presented to change the color of the center button light.

As buttons are pressed, various beeping and musical sounds are emitted from a speaker on the side of the Hub, shown in Figure 1-6. Every press of a button gives a sound through the speaker to provide feedback that a button has been pressed. The different button functions have different sounds. For example, when the Hub is turned on by pressing the center button, there is a series of accelerating clicks followed by a musical chirp.

Figure 1-6. *Sound output is from a speaker on the side of the Hub*

As shown in Figure 1-7, all six sides of the Hub have holes for inserting LEGO pins. There are several kinds of pins, which are discussed in detail in Chapter 3. Larger LEGO building elements can be attached to these pins, as will be seen in the upcoming projects of this book.

Figure 1-7. *Pins can be inserted into opening on all the sides of the Hub*

Exercise: The Motor Spinner

The Robot Inventor and SPIKE Prime sets come with a variety of motors and sensors. These motors and sensors can be quickly identified by their attached cables, which plug into one of the six ports on the Hub. These motors and sensors can be programmed to do all sorts of sophisticated functions, but the Hub also allows control of a motor or sensor by simply plugging it in, without any programming. This feature can be used to activate a motor or change the speed of its rotation. The Motor Spinner in Figure 1-8 demonstrates this plug-and-play feature.

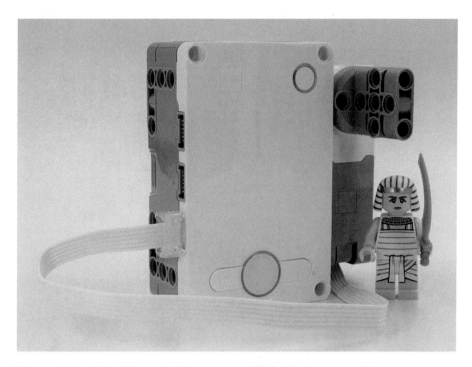

Figure 1-8. *The Motor Spinner uses the Hub to control a motor*

Instructions to build the Motor Spinner are given as follows. All of the parts for this project, and all the projects in this book, are part of the Robot Inventor set.

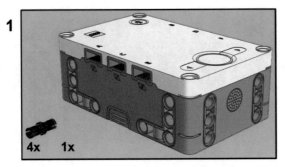

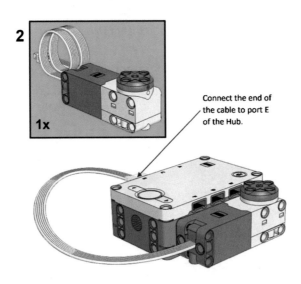

Connect the end of
the cable to port E
of the Hub.

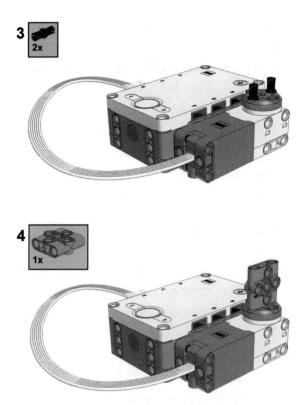

Activating the Motor

To control the Motor Spinner, the first step is to power up the Hub by pressing the center button. The Hub should chirp, and the matrix should display the play symbol. After another press of the center button, a row of lights next to port E should appear with the LED light closest to the port coming on, along with a square of light moving from right to left. This lit-up row indicates that the Hub has recognized the motor. Since port E is used for motor connection, this row of lights is lit up. If, instead, a different port was used, its associated row would light up. Port E is used in this exercise for convenient routing of the cable and in preparation for the following project. A press of the left button once should activate the motor to spin slowly in a clockwise direction. Pressing the right button once should stop the motor. Another press of the right button will make the motor spin slowly counterclockwise. Motor rotation can be sped up by pressing the right button up to ten times. The left button will slow the motor down. With repeated pressing of the left button, the motor will stop, then begin to speed up in a clockwise rotation. When done using the motor, pressing the center button will go back to the home menu, represented by the play symbol on the LED matrix display.

Project: The Distance Spinner

Sensors can also be read by the Hub without programming, much like a motor can be controlled by just plugging it into the Hub. The Distance Spinner project in Figure 1-9 shows how to include a sensor in a project and uses all the techniques of this chapter. The Distance Spinner spins a motor at a speed that depends on how close the Hub is to an object. The closer the object, the faster the motor will spin. Building instructions are given following Figure 1-9. The Distance Spinner is an extension of the Motor Spinner, so the following instructions start after completion of the Motor Spinner in Figure 1-8.

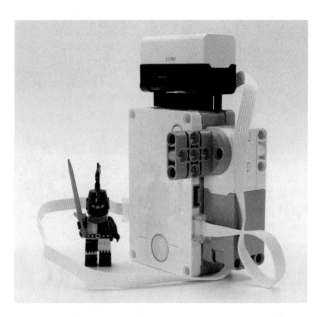

Figure 1-9. *The Distance Spinner will spin faster when objects are closer to the sensor*

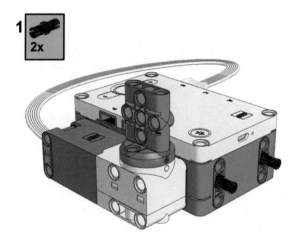

13

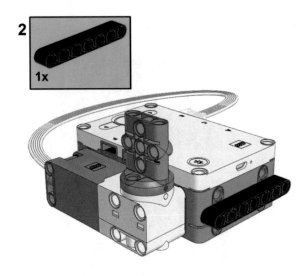

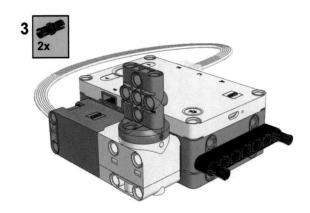

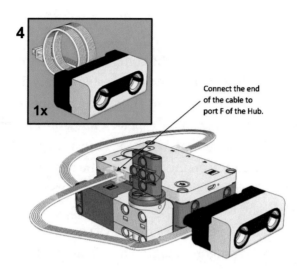

Using the Distance Spinner

After powering up the Hub with a press of the center button, a second press of the center button will activate the Distance Spinner. The lowest row of the LED matrix display should light up on the front panel, indicating that the Hub has recognized the connection of both the Distance Sensor and motor. If an object, such as a wall, is within about 2 m distance away, the motor will spin. A good test is to stand about 2 m away from a wall with the Distance Spinner facing the wall. In moving closer to the wall, the motor spins faster. When done working with the Distance Sensor, a press of the center button will return the user back to the home play symbol on the Hub's LED matrix.

Summary

This chapter introduced the Hub, the computer heart of the Robot Inventor or SPIKE Prime set. The Hub uses a rechargeable battery for power, which can be charged by a USB connection. There are a number of displays on the Hub, including LEDs, as well as a speaker for audio output. Input to the Hub includes several buttons to navigate the front panel control and displays. The center button on the Hub turns the Hub on and off. The Hub offers simple functionality for the motors and sensors without a need to program the Hub, and two quick building projects showed the use of the Hub with the Distance Sensor and a motor. Of course, the Hub is meant to be quite versatile with programming, which Chapter 2 delves into.

CHAPTER 2

Programming

As described in Chapter 1, the Hub can control motors and sensors, with some functionality under control of the Hub's front panel. But the real power of the Hub is that it can host computer programs for sophisticated control of inventions. This chapter will show how to program the Hub. Moreover, the process will be described of how to design and build computer programs, starting from a basic idea to the finished product of code. Programs are coded in the Robot Inventor app on a smart device or computer, then downloaded into the Hub's memory. The Hub can then be disconnected from the host device to work independently. Exercises and the project in this chapter will explain how to install and use the Robot Inventor app, navigate through its functions, and write code in both the Word Blocks and Python computer languages.

Using the Robot Inventor App

Programming the Hub is done in the Robot Inventor app, which can be hosted on a smartphone, tablet, desktop, or laptop computer. Programs developed in the app get downloaded and stored in the Hub's memory, so programs can then be run without connection to a host device.

© Grady Koch 2023
G. Koch, *Learn Engineering with LEGO*, Maker Innovations Series,
https://doi.org/10.1007/978-1-4842-9280-8_2

Installing and Updating the App

Robot Inventor can typically be downloaded from the app store on a particular device, such as the Microsoft Windows Store on a PC computer or the iOS App Store for an Apple Product. A search in the app store for "LEGO MINDSTORMS Robot Inventor" should find the app. Alternatively, the app can be found on the LEGO website at *www.lego.com/en-us/ themes/mindstorms/app*. Running the app should bring up a home screen like Figure 2-1. The first time the app is run, and every so often afterward, a notice may pop up on the screen indicating that an update is available, and directions on the screen will make the update. This update is from LEGO to improve features of the app and fix small problems that are discovered as more people use the app.

The Interface

The largest feature on the home screen, shown in Figure 2-1, is the five example robots that are featured with the Robot Inventor set. Clicking one of these robots will show instructions for building the robot. These robots are fun to build and a good introduction to LEGO MINDSTORMS, but the main interest in this book is on the icons at the bottom of the home screen for home, community, projects, and code.

Figure 2-1. *The home screen for the Robot Inventor app*

- **Home:** Returns to the home screen

- **Community:** Shows extra projects in addition to the five example robots

- **Projects:** Shows a list of saved programs

- **Code:** Opens a new screen in which to write programs

Clicking **Code** accesses the code screen, as in Figure 2-2. There's a lot going on in this screen, which will be covered in detail in this chapter.

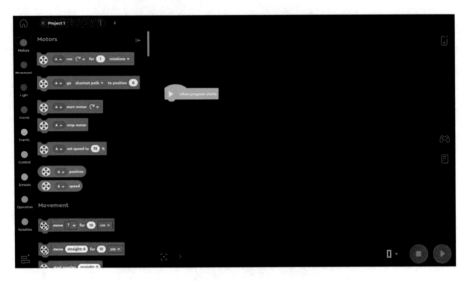

Figure 2-2. *The code screen in the Robot Inventor app*

Connecting the Hub

The Hub gets connected to the app by clicking the small icon in the upper-right corner of the screen. (This icon looks like the Hub's outline.) The screen shown in Figure 2-3 should then appear to prompt the type of connection: USB cable or Bluetooth.

The USB cable comes with the Robot Inventor set and serves two functions of connecting the Hub to the app and charging the Hub's battery. With successful connection, the icon of the Hub in the upper-right corner now has a green dot next to it.

The second option for connection is by Bluetooth, which is useful if the host device doesn't have a USB port, such as smartphone or many tablet computers. Bluetooth is a type of radio communication, so it doesn't require a cable. Clicking the Bluetooth tab at the top of the Connect Hub screen will bring up instructions for making the connection, which involves pressing the button on the Hub's front panel.

Once successfully connected, the app returns to the code screen in Figure 2-2. However, a prompt may appear to update the Hub, as described in the following section.

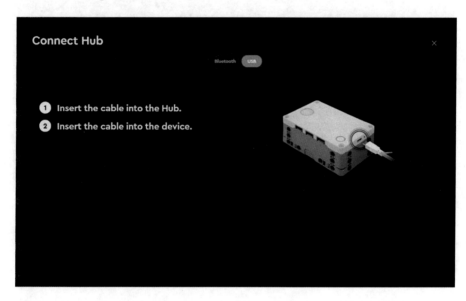

Figure 2-3. *The Connect Hub screen presents two options for connecting the Hub to the Robot Inventor app*

Updating the Hub Operating System

After the Hub is connected to the Robot Inventor app for the first time, a notice is likely to appear to prompt for an update of the Hub's operating system, such as in the screenshot in Figure 2-4. This update will make the Hub run better, with improvements and bug fixes that LEGO releases every few months or so. Clicking **start update** will proceed with loading the update onto the Hub. This update for the Hub is different from the update for the app, but in either case the app will give a pop-up menu when it's time for either update.

Figure 2-4. *The Robot Inventor app will prompt the user when an update is needed to the Hub's operating system*

Exploring the Hub Screen

Once the Hub is connected to the Robot Inventor app and needed updates are done, the Hub icon again should appear in the upper-right corner of the code screen. Clicking this icon will bring up a diagnostic view of the Hub, as reproduced in Figure 2-5. Information at the top of the screen includes the Hub's operating system version and the level of the battery's charge. The purple oval in the upper-right corner will disconnect the Hub from the device running the app. Disconnecting the Hub in this way avoids potential problems with data transfers that could occur if the USB cable was pulled out or Bluetooth abruptly shut off.

Two tabs near the top of the screen are noteworthy: Hardware and Programs. The Hardware tab includes a picture of the Hub, as well as any sensors or motors connected to it and any measurements coming from them. In the example in Figure 2-5, a motor is connected to port A and a Distance Sensor connected to port B. In addition to any external components connected to the Hub, the Hardware tab also displays readings from the built-in Motion Sensor, which indicates the tilt angle, orientation, gyro rate, and acceleration of the Hub. Chapter 7 explores this Motion Sensor in detail, but a quick experiment can be done now by tilting the Hub and watching the yaw, pitch, and roll angle values change.

Figure 2-5. *The Hub screen*

The Programs tab lets the user view and manage the files stored on the Hub. It shows the 20 storage slots available for programs, as well as the name, size, date of creation, and date of last modification of all programs. Programs can also be deleted from this screen, which may occasionally be desired to clear memory space as new programs are developed.

The last important item on the Hub screen is the three-dot icon at the top-right edge. Clicking this feature will bring up a submenu that allows renaming the Hub, resetting the Hub, and updating connected motors. If using more than one Hub, for instance, in working with a school group or team, different names for the Hub can avoid confusion. "Reset hub" is a quick way to delete all the programs on the Hub, so care must be taken to be sure such action is actually desired. "Update motors" starts a set of instructions that checks the motors' operation and calibration, notably related to their reference zero home position (a feature described in Chapter 6). If motors are used often, they can develop problems, which can likely be fixed with this update feature.

Now that a tour of the Hub screen is complete, it's time to develop a program. Clicking the **X** in the upper-right corner of the Hub screen should return the user to the code screen, such as in Figure 2-2.

The Program Design Process

The code screen, shown in Figure 2-2, is where a program is entered. But in implementing a program, entering the code is the last of three parts. The first two parts are algorithm development and flowcharting, which are written out separately from the code screen, such as in a word processing app or even on paper. The reason not to just jump right into coding is that the whole picture of a computer program has to be understood. It'll actually save time and effort to write out the big picture first, in words, of the steps involved in the program. These steps are called an *algorithm*. Then an intermediate component of flowcharting will help translate algorithm steps into code. In the professional world of computer programming, more time is spent debugging and fixing computer code than in writing code. But by taking the time up front to design a computer program with a logical process from an algorithm to a flowchart to code, time and trouble can be saved in the long run. The following sections walk through the process of each of the three parts of the algorithm, flowchart, and code. Then, in the rest of the book, the three parts of the algorithm, flowchart, and code will be used in building projects. As a first example of the program design process, the following exercise has the Hub to spell out a name, beep the speaker, and light up the center button with a specific color.

Writing the Algorithm

An *algorithm* is a set of step-by-step instructions to solve a problem. To start creating an algorithm, the problem or goal should be understood and written out. For example, a goal to achieve could be the following:

> Display my name, emit a beep from the Hub's speaker, and light up my favorite color on the Hub's center button. Keep my favorite color lit up for ten seconds.

Next, the sequence of steps needed to achieve this goal is written out:

1. Start the program.

2. Display the text "Grady" on the Hub's front panel.

3. Beep the Hub's speaker.

4. Set the center button color to blue.

5. Wait for ten seconds.

6. Stop the program.

Of course, the reader can change the code to their own name and favorite color.

Drawing the Flowchart

A *flowchart* is a graphical representation of an algorithm and serves as an intermediate component in implementing the final product of code. The reason to use a flowchart is that it shows how the algorithm flows and how algorithm steps may be interrelated. This flow and interaction of steps matches how to represent instructions in computer languages. Flowcharts use shapes to represent different types of algorithm functions, such as in Table 2-1. These functions include starting and stopping a program, manipulating data, asking for input, providing output, making decisions, and repeating steps with a loop. A flowchart can be sketched on paper for a quick solution or by using the shapes built into most word processors. There are also many apps that are meant for quickly drawing flowcharts.

Table 2-1. *Flowchart Shapes and Functions*

Shape	Name	Description
	Flow direction	Direction of algorithm steps
	Terminal	Beginning or end of an algorithm (usually the first and last steps of an algorithm)
	Process	Instruction to change the value, form, or location of data
	Input/output	Sending of data into or out of the algorithm
	Decision	Question to offer choices in the path of the algorithm
	Looping	Repetition of a set of steps
	Delay	Pause in the algorithm for a specified duration of time
	Connector	Joining of flow paths coming from different directions

The flowchart is a sequence of these shapes joined by arrows. As an example, Figure 2-6 shows a flowchart to match the name and color algorithm laid out in the previous section.

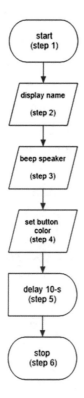

Figure 2-6. *Flowchart for the name and color algorithm*

Writing the Program

Now that a flowchart is written, it's easy to see the commands needed to enter into the code. The Hub can be programmed with two different computer languages in the Robot Inventor app: Word Blocks or Python. Word Blocks is the default language that comes up when the Robot Inventor app is opened to the code screen, such as in Figure 2-2. Commands are entered in Word Blocks by dragging them from the left side of the screen into the center, linking blocks from top to bottom. To program in Python, there's an extra step from the code screen to open a new screen for entering commands, described in a section later. Python is entered by typing lines of code. Deciding on which language to use depends on several factors. If using a smartphone or tablet computer without a keyboard, then Word Blocks is probably a better choice. Using Python requires a lot of typing, which is rather tedious without a keyboard. Word Blocks is easier for a beginner to use and has more built-in commands in the Robot Inventor app. Python is oriented toward more experienced users. The benefit of Python is that it more directly interacts with the Hub, so it can be used for more advanced inventions. Python is widely used outside MINDSTORMS, such as for programming microcontrollers, sophisticated computer programs, and scientific applications. So MINDSTORMS or SPIKE Prime can be a good introduction to building up skill with Python.

In the following sections, and throughout this book, code will be presented in both Word Blocks and Python. This way, the reader can choose whichever computer language is preferred or whichever language is better suited to the type of smart device or computer.

Coding in Word Blocks

Word Blocks is the computer language that appears by default in the code screen, such as in Figure 2-2. Programs are built by clicking a command from the left side of the screen and dragging it to the center part of the screen to link below an existing Word Block. There are many Word Blocks to choose from. They're arranged in pallets of various colors on the left side of the screen, as shown in Figure 2-7, to group the blocks into families that, for example, work with particular motors or sensors. At the bottom of this column of colored circles, there's an icon that looks like an outline of two stacked Word Blocks, which will access Word Block features used to perform advanced functions.

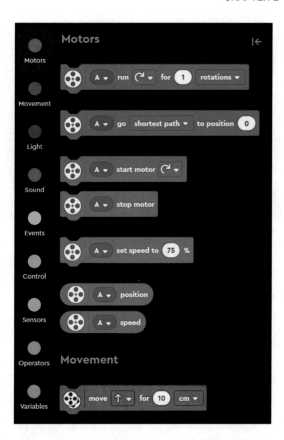

Figure 2-7. *Families of Word Blocks are organized by color*

The code screen has the first block preloaded of when program starts, which starts the program and represents step 1 of any algorithm and the first step in a flowchart. Figure 2-8 shows the insertion of the second command of the flowchart in Figure 2-6 by selecting write from the left side of the screen and dragging it underneath when program starts. The text to get written is entered by clicking the text oval within write and typing in the desired text.

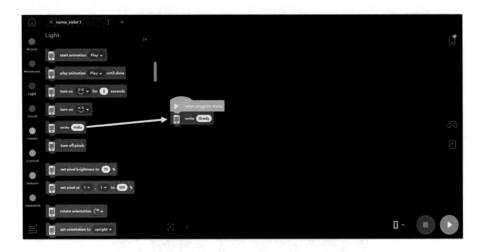

Figure 2-8. *Programs are built in Word Blocks by dragging commands to the center of the screen*

The next steps of the name and color code are added by dragging in a block for each step in the flowchart. Figure 2-9 shows the finished code with all the Word Blocks to be used, but the step-by-step addition of each block is described following Figure 2-9. The Word Blocks code is remarkably similar to the flowchart in Figure 2-6, which shows the utility of a flowchart in implementing code.

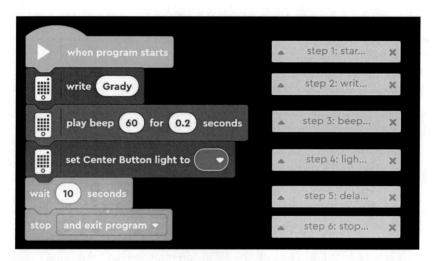

Figure 2-9. *Word Blocks code for the name and color algorithm*

- Step 3: The play beep block makes a sound on the
  Hub's speaker. Inside the block are ovals to click to
  change the values of parameters. In this case, the
  parameter is the musical note of the beep and how long
  it should play. The problem statement (described in a
  previous section) didn't specify what the note should
  be or for how long to play it, so in situations like this the
  programmer can decide such details. For example, the
  default setting of 60 can be used for the musical note.
  The second parameter to input on is the duration of the
  sound, with 0.2 a good starting point.

PROGRAMMING MUSICAL NOTES

Robot Inventor and SPIKE Prime represent musical notes using MIDI notation. The *Musical Instrument Digital Interface* (MIDI) is a way for computers to describe music by assigning notes a number from 0 to 127. For example, MIDI note 60 corresponds to middle C on a piano, and 61 corresponds to C#.

- Step 4: The set Center Button light block controls the light in the center of the Hub. The parameter setting on this block is a drop-down menu of various colors. Blue is selected in this example, but the reader can select their favorite.

- Step 5: The wait block pauses the program to give a little time to admire the color on the center button. The flowchart and algorithm call this step "delay," since this is the standard term used when making flowcharts, but in Word Blocks code, it's called wait. The two terms mean the same thing. The problem statement specified a ten-second delay, so 10 is set for the delay parameter.

- Step 6: The stop block closes out the program and lets the Hub know that it's done for now. A program would still work without this block, but it's a good practice to gracefully end a program. This way, the computer knows it can go back to a state of being ready for another program to be run. Such a stop block is used in all the programs of this book. From the drop-down menu, a selection and exit program tells the Hub that the program is really done. There are other options that come up in more advanced projects, but and exit program is a good choice for most projects.

Writing Comments

Another feature of writing code is to add comments to the code. These comments are not commands, but an explanation to help remember what the program or command line does. Comments are helpful when looking back at an old program that might be used again. The comments will quickly explain what the program does and how it works, so time can be saved when reusing the code. Also, several people may be working on a project, and having all the comments in place will help other people figure out what another person might have done. Word Blocks includes a way to add comments in the code area, implemented as light yellow blocks to the right of the Word Block commands.

Figure 2-10 shows a comment being added as the code is developed, which can be initiated by right-clicking anywhere in the area where the code is being built and selecting **Add Comment** from the pop-up menu. The comment box will then appear on the screen, looking like a sticky note, where text can be entered. The comment box can be as big as needed, so there's lots of room for detail. For example, in commenting on step 1 of the code in Figure 2-10, there's an explanation of the code's file name, programmer's name, and date. Then the problem statement is written to explain what the program does. When the comment is complete, clicking the triangle in the upper left-hand corner of the comment box will collapse the block to a convenient size on the screen. The complete entry in the comment box can later be read by clicking this triangle. A comment for every command in the code can be useful, as has been done in Figure 2-9 with a comment off to the right of each Word Block step. Each comment includes the step number of the algorithm to see how the code relates to the algorithm steps.

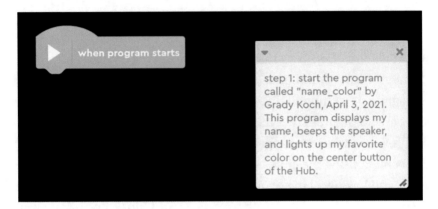

Figure 2-10. *Comment box for step 1*

Once comments are all added, the complete program needs to be saved on the host computer or smart device from the toolbar at the top of the screen.

Coding in Python

Python is a text-based programming language that requires typing in commands with a very specific syntax. While the following projects are good examples, a complete introduction to Python is outside the scope of this book. The full details on Python can be found at *python.org*.

To start programming in Python, a new program is initiated on the code screen, either by clicking the + symbol at the top of the screen or by selecting **File ➤ New Project** in the toolbar. A pop-up menu should appear, as in Figure 2-11. Clicking **Python** and then **Create** will bring up the screen in Figure 2-12 for entering code.

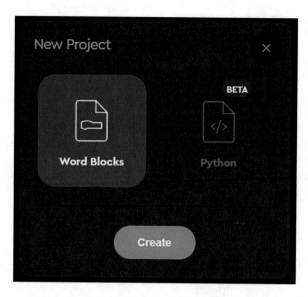

Figure 2-11. *The New Project menu presents options for Word Blocks or Python*

Figure 2-12. *The Python coding screen opens up with several lines of code automatically entered*

The Complete Code

The complete Python program for the name and color algorithm is shown as follows, which will be explained in detail in the following sections. The first four lines of code automatically appear on the code screen and need not be typed in.

```python
from mindstorms import MSHub, Motor, ...
from mindstorms.control import wait_for_seconds, ...
from mindstorms.operator import greater_than, ...
import math
import hub
from sys import exit

#Create your objects here.
myhub = MSHub()

# Program "name_color". Display name, beep speaker, light up
center button
myhub.light_matrix.write('Grady')
myhub.speaker.beep(60,0.2)
myhub.status_light.on('blue')
wait_for_seconds(10)
exit()
```

Comments in Python are written by preceding them with a # sign. All text after # is part of the comment, which the code screen automatically changes to purple text to make it easier to see. Code gets saved and given a file name by clicking **File ➤ Save As** in the toolbar at the top of the screen.

Importing Code

The first four lines of code are included whenever the Python coding screen is opened and should be kept in place as they are. These lines feature from and import statements, which are used to include external code that allows working with all the components of Robot Inventor or SPIKE Prime, such as motors, sensors, and the Hub:

```
1from mindstorms import MSHub, Motor, ...
from mindstorms.control import wait_for_seconds, ...
from mindstorms.operator import greater_than, ...
2import math
3import hub
4from sys import exit
```

The from statement references various packages, called mindstorms, mindstorms.control, and mindstorms.operator. A *package* is a folder of files that contains extra features for using Python, called modules. These *modules* are files containing statements and definitions that help perform specific tasks. Within the module's code, these statements and definitions may take up many lines, but can be referenced in a program with just a single line of code, making the program more efficient. Modules to include are indicated with the import statement. For example, the first line in the code calls many modules, including MSHub, Motor, and others 1 from the mindstorms package.

Some modules are used often and so aren't contained in a specific package. These more common modules, like math, can be called with just import 2.

Two more lines are needed to add to the list of modules. The hub module provides a way to interact with various features on the Hub 3, and the exit module, stored in the sys package, allows a smooth end to a program 4. These two extra import statements are added to all the programs in this book.

Creating an Object and Assigning It to a Variable

The following line shows the creation of an object:

```
myhub = MSHub()
```

An *object*, in programming terminology, is a collection of data and functions that act on the data. Here, the code MSHub() creates an object containing the data and functions associated with the internal workings of the Hub. MSHub() comes from a module within the mindstorms package that was imported in the very first line of code.

Also, this object has been assigned to the variable myhub. A *variable* is a name for a piece of data. An object can be given a variable name, so long as it doesn't conflict with other names in a program. Now the data and functions of the Hub can be accessed by referring to the variable myhub. In later chapters, objects will be used to represent the data for motors or sensors.

The code written so far forms the beginning of all Python programs in this book and so will be seen again many times.

Displaying Text on the Hub Screen

Now that the basics of the program are out of the way, action can be taken to implement steps 2 through 5 of the name and color algorithm. Step 2 is to display a name on the LED matrix of the Hub's front panel. Due to the power of Python modules, this can be done with one line of code:

```
myhub.light_matrix.write('Grady')
```

This code uses a function called light_matrix.write(). A *function* in Python is code that performs a specific task. In this case, the function spells out text on the front panel. Functions are saved in modules; in this case, the function used here is in the MSHub module. When the myhub object was created, access was gained to its functions, one of which is `light_matrix.write()`. To use the function, a command is written of the object's name (`myhub` in this case), then a period, then the function's name (`light_matrix.write()` in this case).

Certain functions, like this one, accept parameters or optional values specified within parentheses. In this case, the parameter is whatever text is to be spelled out. This text is in quotation marks, which tells the program that it's working with a data type called a string. A *string* is essentially text, which can be thought of as a sequence of characters that can be printed, such as letters, numbers, punctuation marks, or whitespace (the space between words).

Beeping the Hub Speaker

Step 3 of the algorithm is to beep the Hub's speaker. This can be done using a function, too:

`myhub.speaker.beep(60,0.2)`

Just as in the previous step, this function is called by referencing the `myhub` object, followed by the function's name, `speaker.beep()`. The note and duration of the beep are specified inside the parentheses. In this case, a note has been assigned a value of 60 for a duration of 0.2 seconds. (Notes are defined by MIDI notation, as described earlier.) The numbers passed into the function don't have quotation marks around them, because they represent numerical values, not text like the string used in step 2.

Setting the Center Button Light

Next, another function sets the center button light on the Hub to a specified color:

`myhub.status_light.on('blue')`

The name of the function for controlling the center light is `status_light_on()`. The color choice is written in quotation marks inside the parentheses. Possible choices include azure, blue, cyan, green, orange, pink, red, violet, yellow, and white.

Waiting Ten Seconds

The next task is to delay the program for a time period of ten seconds to give time to admire the color on the center button. This delay is accomplished with a function called `wait_for_seconds()`:

```
wait_for_seconds(10)
```

This function looks a little different than earlier functions, with no reference to an object or variable. In other words, there's no variable name or period before this function name, since this particular function is not grouped within an object. The number of seconds to delay the program gets inserted inside the parentheses of the function.

Ending the Program

The algorithm ends with the `exit()` function:

```
exit()
```

This function lets the Hub know that the program is over. Now the Hub can go into a standby mode and get ready for whatever might be coming next. The program will still work without this function by ending the program when it gets to the last line of code. However, it's a good practice to formally stop and exit a program.

Downloading and Running Code

Once code is finished, it's time to load it into the Hub using the three icons in the lower-right corner of the code screen as in Figure 2-13. This procedure is the same regardless of whether the code was written in Word Blocks or Python.

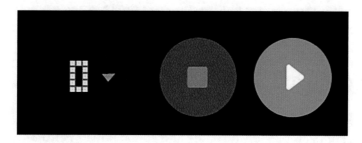

Figure 2-13. *Icons for loading and running programs are at the lower-right section of the code screen*

The first icon includes a number that represents the slot on the Hub in which to save the program. There are 20 possible slots, numbered from 0 to 19, allowing many programs to be stored in the Hub's memory. Upon clicking the program number icon, a pop-up menu will appear for selecting the slot number. (Slot 0 is selected in Figure 2-13.) This same pop-up window allows download of the code onto the Hub without running the program. The program then gets run from the front panel of the Hub.

If it's preferred to both download and run the program in one step, the play icon can be found at the far right of the group of icons. This option is more convenient, but the two-step process can be useful if it's desired to closely watch results as the code runs. For example, if running a program for the first time that involves complex motor action, it might be desired to check for a coding mistake that causes a motor to run wild. In this case, it would be preferable to download the program from the code screen, take a moment to shift attention to the Hub, and run the program from its front panel. The remaining icon to consider is the stop icon, which halts execution of the program. Such a stop may be warranted if a mistake is found or if something about the code takes a long time to run.

After the program is saved into the Hub's memory, the Hub can be disconnected from the app. Pressing the center button of the Hub will run the program. If needed, another press of the center button will abort the program. If multiple programs are stored on the Hub, the left and right buttons will scroll through all the programs stored on the Hub.

Debugging and Troubleshooting

It's quite common for there to be a mistake in code when it's run for the first time. For example, for the name and color code in Word Blocks, the name may have been spelled wrong or the wrong color was selected for display on the center button light. When this sort of thing happens, the programmer can go back to the code, make corrections, and try the program again.

Python is easier to make a mistake with than Word Blocks. A command may have been typed in with the wrong spelling or the ( ) forgotten after many commands. Another common mistake is in trying to use a function that wasn't properly called. The Python code screen includes an area where problems will be identified and described to give a suggestion on how to fix the problem. As shown in Figure 2-14, this error message area is near the bottom of the screen that can be opened by clicking the >- icon. In the example in Figure 2-14, the code for the name and color algorithm was changed to intentionally add in the mistake in line 12 of misspelling write with writ. When this code is run, the program will fail because of the mistake. The program halts when it gets to this mistake and gives the error message seen in Figure 2-14. The error message indicates that there's a mistake in spelling write. Aside from the error message in the app's code screen, the Hub will also indicate that there's a problem by blinking red on the center button light.

```
11
12 myhub.light_matrix.writ('Grady')
13 myhub.speaker.beep(60,0.2)
14 myhub.status_light.on('blue')
15 wait_for_seconds(10)
```

Figure 2-14. *Python debugging error messages are in a monitor at the bottom of the code screen*

Project: The Dance Floor

Now having experience with the Robot Inventor app and seeing how computer programs are designed, programming techniques of a little more complexity can be explored with the Dance Floor. The Dance Floor creates a miniature dance floor for LEGO minifigures, as shown in Figure 2-15. The Dance Floor can also be used as a metronome for practicing with a musical instrument. Whereas the name and color program earlier in this chapter was a straightforward series of steps, the Dance Floor incorporates programming techniques for the use of variables, decision making, and loops. Variables are values that can change, in this case to count from 1 to 5. Decision making in a program provides multiple paths of operation, in this case presenting two paths that depend on whether a button on the Hub is pressed. Loops in a program repeat some actions, in this case to cycle through colors on the center button, draw a diagonal line of lights on the LED matrix, and click a musical beat.

Figure 2-15. *The front panel of the Hub can be used as a dance floor for minifigures*

To start designing our program, the problem statement defines what the Dance Floor should accomplish:

> Create a musical beat that plays on the Hub's speaker at five beats per second. On each beat, change the color of the center button and light up pixels on the LED matrix. Start by lighting the pixel in the upper-left corner, then light up the pixel diagonally adjacent to it. When all the pixels in the diagonal have been lit, begin again in the upper-left pixel. Include the ability to stop the beat by pressing either the left or right button.

The following algorithm can achieve the task laid out in this problem statement. It uses a variable called count to represent values of 1 through 5, each of which corresponds to a new color on the front button and a different pixel to light up on the LED matrix. A loop in step 3 repeats the sound and light action, which gets halted only if the left or right button is pressed on the Hub's front panel.

1. Start the program.

2. Define the variable count = 1.

3. Create a loop that repeats unless the left or right button is pressed. If either button is pressed, skip to step 12.

4. Set the center button to the color represented by count.

5. Beep the Hub's speaker.

6. Light up the LED matrix pixel at coordinates count, count.

7. Delay for 0.2 seconds. This delay sets the timing between beats.

8. Increase the value of count by 1.

9. Test to determine if count is greater than 5. If yes, proceed to step 10. If no, return to step 3.

10. Reset the value of count to 1.

11. Turn off all pixels on the LED matrix.

12. Stop the program.

The preceding algorithm includes steps that repeat and a decision point that can be a little difficult to follow when expressed as words. The power of a flowchart as the next component in developing code is to provide a visualization of loops and decisions, where the flow of the program can go in different directions. With the flow visualized in a flowchart, the next step of coding will become easier to write. The flowchart for the Dance Floor is shown in Figure 2-16. Step 3 starts a loop that executes through to step 11, unless a button is pressed on the Hub. Pressing a button exits the loop and then proceeds to stop the program. Loops are easy to see in a flowchart by the long arrows that direct flow back to an earlier step. The decision in the algorithm, step 9, is drawn in a flowchart with a diamond shape. Arrows flow from the decision to represent the possible outcomes from the decision, in this case deciding if the *count* variable has reached a value of more than 5.

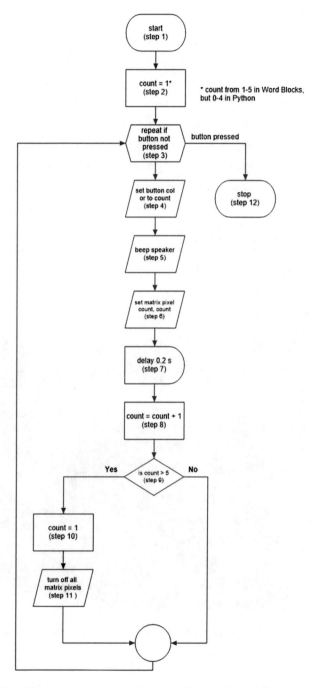

Figure 2-16. *Flowchart for the Dance Floor algorithm*

The Dance Floor algorithm can be coded in either Word Blocks or Python, with the code for each language given in the following sections. Handling variables, loops, and decisions are built in to either programming language, but with some minor differences. For example, the rows and columns of the LED matrix are represented by a number of 1–5 in Word Blocks, but 0–4 in Python. So if moving back and forth between the two languages, a little adjustment may be needed to the way things are done. But in either programming language, the basic structure is the same as developed in the flowchart step.

The Word Blocks Code

Figure 2-17 shows the Dance Floor program written in Word Blocks. Each step in the flowchart corresponds to a Word Block, as labeled with the comments. Particular Word Blocks to note are as follows.

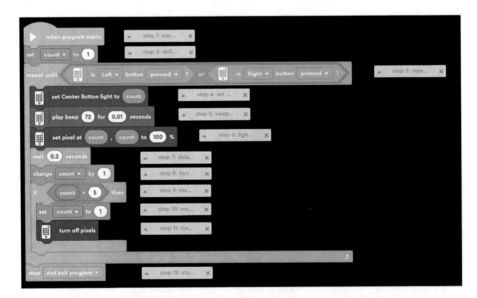

Figure 2-17. *Word Blocks code for the Dance Floor algorithm*

- Step 2: The set count block defines a variable and sets its initial value. Programs typically give variables descriptive names that make it clear what the variable represents. In this case, the value of the count variable will range from 1 to 5. Variables are created in Word Blocks by clicking the orange circle menu labeled Variables. A pop-up menu should then appear, as shown in Figure 2-18, where the name of the new variable is entered. After clicking OK, any variables created will appear as choices in Word Blocks under the Variables menu. One such place to find a variable loaded into a block in the Variables menu is the set Word Block, which can be left here at drop-down menu selection for count. The initial assignment of the value for the variable inside the parameter oval should be given a value of 1.

Figure 2-18. *The new variable menu*

- Step 3: The `repeat until` block sets up a loop that
  repeats indefinitely until a certain condition is met. In
  this case, the condition is that a button is pressed on
  the Hub. In other words, pressing a button will stop the
  loop. Loops in Word Blocks are two horizontal yellow
  bars with a space between them, into which the blocks
  to be repeated are inserted. The hexagon-shaped
  parameter entry area indicates the condition by which
  the loop will repeat, in this case an `or` Word Block,
  which can be found under the Operators group of
  blocks. The `or` block contains two hexagon parameter
  entry areas, which should be filled with `is Left
  Button pressed` and `is Right Button pressed`. Now, if
  either of these conditions is met, the loop will stop.

- Step 4: The `set Center Button light to` block,
  which goes inside the loop, displays a new color on the
  Hub's light. The color is represented here by the `count`
  variable; as the count progresses, the center button
  light will change colors. Color is usually selected from
  a drop-down menu in this block, but in this case a
  number is used as represented by the `count` variable.
  The `count` variable can be found in the Variables menu
  on the left side of the screen.

- Step 5: The `play beep` block makes a sound on the
  Hub's speaker to create a musical beat. A MIDI note of
  72 produces a pleasant sound and is a good starting
  point for experimentation. Since the note is serving as a
  musical beat, its duration should be short, like `0.01`.

- Step 6: The `set pixel at` block lights up a pixel on
  the Hub's LED matrix. A particular pixel is specified
  by its row and column numbers. Since the problem

statement indicated that a diagonal line be lit up, the following row and column pairs accomplish this: 1,1; 2,2; 3,3; 4,4; and 5,5. These numbers for the rows and columns are the same as the value of the count variable, so this variable can be used to indicate which pixel to light up. As the count progresses when the loop repeats, the next pixel in the diagonal line will be lit. The variable count can be found at the left side of the screen, to be dragged into the pixel parameter numbers in set pixel at. The brightness setting at the default value of 100% gives a bright display.

- Step 7: The wait block delays the action before the loop starts over again. This time delay sets the beep's tempo, which the problem statement specified to be five beats per second. This tempo corresponds to a 0.2-second delay between beats, so 0.2 is entered in the parameter oval.

- Step 8: The change count by block increases the value of the count variable by 1. As a result, when the loop restarts, this variable will have increased. With a new value for count, the color will change on the center button, and the next pixel will light up.

- Step 9: The if block presents a condition—it checks whether the count variable has exceeded a value of 5. If so, any Word Blocks contained inside the if block will run, resetting the count variable to a value of 1. If count is 5 or less, no change is made to the count variable. This greater-than conditional test goes into the hexagon-shaped condition parameter, with a > block from the Operators menu.

- Step 10: The set count to block goes inside the if
  block to reset the count variable since it has exceeded a
  value of 5.

- Step 11: The turn off pixels block blanks out the LED
  matrix. This step resets the diagonal of pixels lit up on
  the matrix so it can begin again when the loop repeats.

A useful feature of the Robot Inventor app can be seen by running the Dance Floor program with the host computer or smart device still connected to the Hub. Clicking the card icon on the right side of the screen will bring up a window with two tabs. Clicking the **Monitor** tab, as in Figure 2-19, will show the current values of any variables involved in the code that is running. For the Dance Floor program, the value of the count variable should update as the loop runs, incrementing from 1 to 5 then repeating. This monitor can be helpful in debugging code if a problem arises, because it allows a verification that variables are behaving as expected.

The loop used here repeats quickly, so the variable also updates quickly in the monitor. If having trouble seeing the variable value with the fast update, the loop can be slowed by changing the wait block in step 7 to have a longer time value than 0.2 seconds.

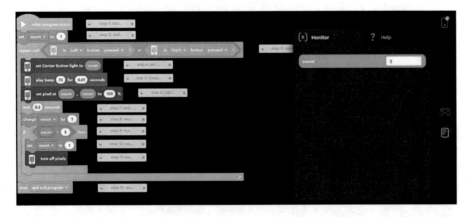

Figure 2-19. *A monitor in the code screen allows viewing of variable values as the program runs*

The Python Code

The following Python code is the completed Dance Floor program:

```
1from mindstorms import MSHub, Motor, ...
from mindstorms.control import wait_for_seconds, ...
from mindstorms.operator import greater_than, ...
import math
import hub
from sys import exit

# Create your objects here.
2myhub = MSHub()

# Program "dance_floor".  Beep musical beat, change button
color, light matrix.
count = 0
while True:
    if myhub.left_button.is_pressed() or myhub.right_button.
    is_pressed():
        exit()
    hub.led(count)
    myhub.speaker.beep(72,0.01)
    myhub.light_matrix.set_pixel(count,count)
    wait_for_seconds(0.2)
    count = count + 1
    if count > 4:
        count = 0
        myhub.light_matrix.off()
```

The program begins by importing modules 1 and creating the myhub object 2, as described earlier in the chapter for the name and color program. The following sections describe coding the remaining steps of the algorithm.

Defining a Variable

A variable represents a numerical value that will change as the program runs. Variables are often given names that suggest what data they represent. In this case, the variable will increase in value from 0 to 4 as the program runs, so count is a good representative name for it:

```
count = 0
```

The variable is created by assigning a value to it with an equals sign.

Beginning the Loop and Checking for a Button Press

The program next sets up a loop to run until the user presses a button on the Hub's front panel. There are several kinds of loops in Python. Here, a loop is used that repeats infinitely using a while True: statement:

```
while True:
    if myhub.left_button.is_pressed() or myhub.right_button.
    is_pressed():
        exit()
```

The while statement checks if the condition after it is true, and since the condition is declared to be True, the loop will run indefinitely. In other words, True is always true, so the while loop will run forever, unless something within the loop interrupts it. This statement has a colon (:) at the end of it, which is required.

All lines of code within the loop must be indented at the same distance. Indentation is critical in writing Python code. If the following line of code wasn't indented, it wouldn't be part of the group of statements that run inside the loop.

The first statement in the loop checks to see if a button has been pressed on the Hub. This check is implemented with an if statement. If the condition of the if statement is met, any following lines of code that are indented will run. If the condition isn't met, those indented lines won't run. Indentation can be seen here again to be critical. In this case, the indented line would exit the program, step 12 of the algorithm.

To specify a condition for the if statement, the functions left_button.is_pressed and right_button.is_pressed are used, which, as their names suggest, check with the Hub to see if a button has been activated. These two functions are combined with an or, which means that activation of either button will serve to satisfy the if condition.

Setting the Center Button Light Color

Still within the loop, the Hub's center button light gets set with the led() function:

```
hub.led(count)
```

As a parameter, the function accepts a number that corresponds to a color. In this case, the number is represented by the count variable, whose values increment from 0 to 4. Therefore, each time the variable increments, a new color will appear on the center button light. This function is in the hub module and shouldn't be confused with the myhub object.

Beeping the Hub Speaker

Next, the Hub's speaker gets beeped with the speaker.beep() function:

```
myhub.speaker.beep(72,0.01)
```

This function takes two parameters, separated by a comma: a number indicating the note to play and another number indicating the duration of the note. The choice of MIDI note is up to the programmer, since the problem statement didn't specify the note to use. Since the beep in this program is a musical beat, it should be quick; hence, a short duration of 0.01 seconds is used.

Lighting Up a Pixel

As each beat is played, a new pixel on the Hub's LED matrix should light up along a diagonal path, beginning from the upper-left corner (0,0) to the lower-right corner (4,4). This function takes two numbers inside the parentheses as x, y coordinates to light up a pixel at column x (starting from the left) and row y (starting from the top). The pixel's row and column values correspond to the various values of the count variable, so we can use the count variable in a light_matrix.set_pixel() function:

```
myhub.light_matrix.set_pixel(count,count)
```

Setting the Tempo with a Delay

Since the problem statement called for a tempo of five beats per second, a delay of 0.2 seconds is called for. This tempo can be implemented with the wait_for_seconds() function:

```
wait_for_seconds(0.2)
```

As a result, the color on the center button light and the pixel lit up on the LED matrix will remain for 0.2 seconds before the loop runs again.

Incrementing a Variable

Now that the loop has beeped and updated the lights on the Hub, the count variable should be updated for the next iteration of the loop. A variable can be updated in Python by redefining its value with an equals sign. In this case, 1 is added to the previous value of count:

```
count = count + 1
```

Checking the Value of a Count

After the count variable has been updated, a check needs to be made on the new value of count to see if it has exceeded a value of 4. The problem statement for the Dance Floor asks for 5 beats and for 5 pixels on the LED matrix to be lit, and the count variable keeps track of the actions that take place in a cycle of 5. The count starts at 0 (not 1), so the final value of count should be 4. The value of count is tested with an if statement:

```
if count > 4:
    count = 0
    myhub.light_matrix.off()
```

The if statement checks whether a condition is true or not. In this case, the condition is if the variable count is greater than 4. If this condition is true, then the indented lines of code after the : will be executed. These indented lines reset count to 0 and switch off all the pixels on the LED matrix. If the answer to the condition is false, then no action is taken on the value of count.

Summary

This chapter described how to connect the Hub to the Robot Inventor app. This app allows programming the Hub, but also has functions to update the operating system of the Hub. These updates occasionally come from LEGO to improve the performance of the Hub. The app also has features to check the Hub's battery level and check for correct operation of motors and sensors that are connected to the Hub. To program with the Robot Inventor app, two different programming languages can be used: Word Blocks or Python. Word Blocks is simpler to use than Python and a good starting point for users new to programming. Since it's graphical, Word Blocks is easy to use from a smartphone or tablet computer that doesn't have a keyboard. Python allows for more advanced programming techniques and so may appeal to users already experienced with programming. But before writing code, better results and time savings are likely in the long run by first designing the program's algorithm and flowchart. An algorithm is a step-by-step explanation, written out in words, of how a program will solve the problem. The steps of the algorithm are then expressed graphically in a flowchart, which shows how the algorithm flows through its steps. Then code is writen based on the flowchart, usually with one line of code corresponding to one step of the flowchart. Two example programs in this chapter worked through the design process to control the Hub. For each example program, the last component of writing code can be done in either Word Blocks or Python.

Word Blocks includes many blocks dedicated to controlling the Hub and will be seen in later chapters for working with sensors and motors. In Python, functions are used to work with the Hub. Several coding techniques were shown, including using variables to represent values that can change as a program runs, loops to repeat action multiple times, and conditionals to present multiple options a program can take.

CHAPTER 3

Building Elements

The Robot Inventor and SPIKE Prime sets come with a large pile of building elements, and it may not be obvious to know where to start with all these bits and pieces. This chapter will describe how to use these liftarms, pins, axles, bushes, and connectors. The reasoning behind all of various features of these pieces will be explored by building example structures and devices. In the process, important building techniques are demonstrated, such as creating triangles to make structures stronger and designing mechanical linkages to enable motion. Another exercise involves the use of connectors to build interesting symmetrical objects. The chapter projects, a universal joint and an eccentric, show how to solve a commonly encountered problem: accommodating power sources that involve a rotating shaft.

Liftarms

The building of structures and devices using the Robot Inventor or SPIKE Prime set is based on *liftarms*, shown in their several varieties in Figure 3-1. Some liftarms are straight, some are bent, some are shaped like letters of the alphabet, and some are rectangles. Liftarms are meant to be attached to each other with pins, described in a following section. This connection arrangement is what distinguishes liftarms from LEGO *beams*—a beam, shown in Figures 3-2a and 3-2b, attached to a liftarm, has studs on top so that they can be stacked on top of each other. Beams and liftarms represent two different styles of building: studded (using beams)

© Grady Koch 2023
G. Koch, *Learn Engineering with LEGO*, Maker Innovations Series,
https://doi.org/10.1007/978-1-4842-9280-8_3

and studless (using liftarms). Some LEGO builders prefer to build in one of these two styles. And some LEGO fans tend to combine the two styles. The Robot Inventor and SPIKE Prime sets use the studless style, building with liftarms, so the studless style is used throughout this book. However, Figure 3-2 provides ideas for connecting liftarms to beams, for possibly combining Robot Inventor or SPIKE Prime parts with other LEGO bricks.

Figure 3-1. *Liftarms come in straight lines, bent lines, letters of the alphabet, and rectangles*

Designs using Robot Inventor and SPIKE Prime use the studless style of LEGO building. But if the use of studded pieces, like LEGO System bricks or Technic beams, is desired, there are several ways to make this connection shown in Figure 3-2. One way, shown in Figure 3-2a, is to simply press a liftarm onto a beam. However, this connection is not very strong. So an alternate is to join a liftarm and beam side by side using pins, as in Figure 3-2b. Still another option is to use special bricks that combine stud and studless connections—one such special brick comes in the Robot Inventor set, shown in Figure 3-2c, that has a pin on one side and studs on the other side.

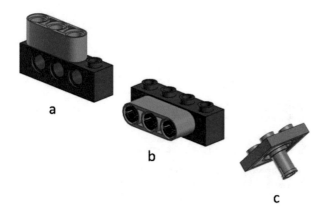

Figure 3-2. *Techniques for joining studded and studless bricks*

Straight Liftarms

Liftarms come in several shapes and sizes, with the most common being straight line liftarms—Figure 3-3 shows these straight liftarms that come in the Robot Inventor set. Different lengths are available, ranging from 2 to 15 holes long. Aside from the 2-hole-long liftarm, straight liftarms come in odd numbers of lengths. So there is no such thing as an 8-, 10-, or 12-hole-long straight liftarm.

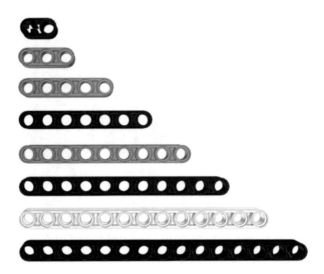

Figure 3-3. *Straight liftarms come in lengths ranging from 2 to 15 holes long*

Bent Liftarms

A design may require to build along different directions, as opposed to attaching things all in a line. For such multidirectional applications, liftarms also come in the bent and letter-shaped varieties shown in Figure 3-4, all of which are in the Robot Inventor set. The longest bent liftarm turns through a right angle, which is useful for building along lines that are perpendicular to each other. The other two bent liftarms turn through an angle of 53.13 degrees, which is useful for building triangular structures, as will be seen later in this chapter. Aside from these bent pieces, letter-shaped pieces also come in useful for building structures. There are L-shaped liftarms, in two sizes, as well as H-shaped and T-shaped liftarms. These letter-shaped pieces will be used in several designs of this book.

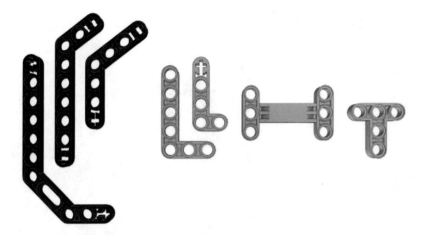

Figure 3-4. *Liftarms also come in bent and letter shapes*

Rectangular Liftarms

Another type of liftarm is rectangular designs, as pictured in Figure 3-5. The larger rectangles, which measure 11 × 15 and 7 × 11 holes long, are useful for the base of a structure or the chassis of a vehicle. The small rectangle, 5 × 7, comes in handy to hold a sensor or motor.

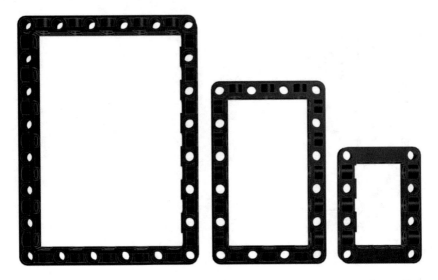

Figure 3-5. *Several sizes of rectangular liftarms come in the Robot Inventor set*

Connecting Liftarms

The holes in liftarms allow them to be joined with other pieces. Some of these holes are round, allowing insertion of a *pin*. Others are cross-shaped to accommodate an *axle*. The main difference between pin and axle connections is that pins allow rotation of the connected parts, whereas an axle will prevent rotation. As pins are more common, most of the openings found in liftarms are round. Rectangular and letter-shaped liftarms have no axle holes at all, and bent liftarms have axle openings at their ends only. Among straight liftarms, only the two-hole-long liftarm has an axle hole.

Pins

Pins come in several varieties, as shown in Figure 3-6. An important feature of pins is if they may have friction ridges, bumps along the surface of the pin. Pins come in varieties with (#2, 4, 6, 8, 9, 10, 11, and 12 in

Figure 3-6) and without (#1, 3, 5, and 7 in Figure 3-6) friction ridges, meant for use in situations to control how easy it is to rotate a pin that has been inserted into a liftarm.

Figure 3-6. *Varieties of pins*

To feel the difference that friction ridges can make, Figure 3-7 shows an exercise to insert a pin with friction ridges and a pin without friction ridges side by side in a liftarm. Spinning each of these installed pin should show that the one without friction ridges spins freely, but the one with friction ridges will only turn with effort. So if a design calls for liftarms to be freely rotating when connected together, a pin without friction ridges will accomplish this.

Figure 3-7. *Pins with friction ridges (left) resist rotation, while those without friction ridges (right) rotate feely*

Pins come in a longer length, such as #6, 7, and 8 in Figure 3-6, for situations in which there's a need to go through three liftarms. Certain pins are designed to adapt axle openings (like #4, 5, and 8 in Figure 3-6) or to a perpendicular pin (like #10 and 11). Others adapt to a stop bush (like #9), which is useful to grab hold of a pin for easy removal. Still others adapt to a tow ball (like #12), useful for connecting a rubber band to a structure or to block against rotation of a liftarm past a certain angle. Pins will be used in these ways throughout the projects in this book.

Axles and Bushes

Some of the pins in Figure 3-6 have axles on one end, meant to join pieces with a pin on one side and axle on the other side. But very often there's a need to join the axle ends of two liftarms or connect to a motor or a gear. It may even be needed to connect devices that are separated by some distance, so axles come in several different lengths. Figure 3-8 summarizes the types of axles that come in the Robot Inventor set. Axles range in length from 2 to 12 long. Some axles are plain, but some have additional features built into them, such as a stop, like the axles labeled (#3, 5, 6, 8, 9, and 13 in Figure 3-8), which serves to keep the axle from sliding past a certain point. Some stops are on the end of an axle (#3, 6, 8, and 13 in Figure 3-8), and some stops are somewhere along the middle length of the axle (#5 and 9 in Figure 3-8). The 2-long axle (#1 in Figure 3-8) has notches in it that helps in removing the axle by giving a place to get a fingernail into the axle. Otherwise, these short axles can be difficult to remove. The colors of axles can help to quickly find the particular length called for in building instructions, but for added clarity the building instructions in this book will often have a number in a yellow square next to the axle to indicate length.

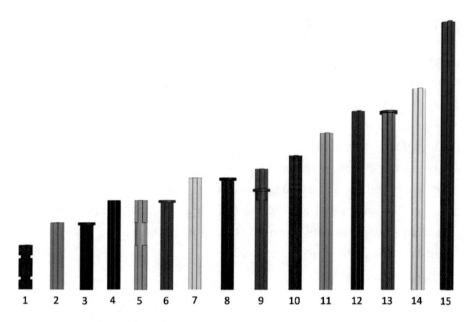

Figure 3-8. *Varieties of axles*

A piece sometimes used with an axle is known as a *bush*, which slides onto an axle. Bushes can be used as a spacer for an axle to keep parts separated and from rubbing together. Or a bush placed on the end of an axle can serve as a lock to keep the axle from sliding. Figure 3-9 shows two kinds of bushes that come with the Robot Inventor set—a full-size bush and a half-size.

Figure 3-9. *Bushes slide onto axles to act as spacers or locks*

Exercise: Triangular Structures

Liftarms, joined together by pins and axles, are the basis for LEGO structures. Figure 3-10 shows an example liftarm structure, called the Triangle Trick, that takes advantage of bent liftarms to incorporate triangular shapes. Triangles are important in building, because they offer the best performance in strength and handling a heavy load. A triangle is stronger than any other shape for sturdiness. But there's a trick in getting a triangle to fit within the usual up-and-down, side-to-side layout of LEGO building. The secret to this trick is in the angle that bent liftarms are at, that is, 53.13 degrees. The Triangle Trick shows how to use this angle with the instructions following Figure 3-10.

Figure 3-10. *The Triangle Trick takes advantage of the angle of a bent liftarm to strengthen a structure*

1

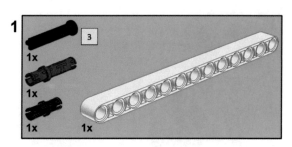

2

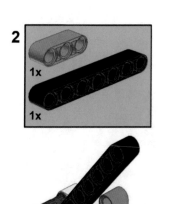

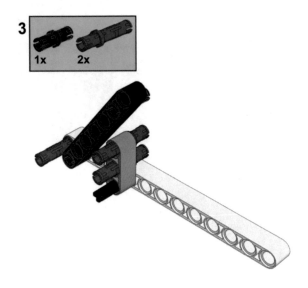

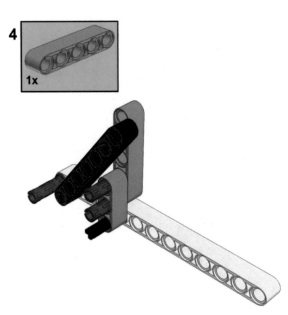

A pause in building is warranted to examine the triangle built after step 4. As diagrammed in Figure 3-11, this is a right triangle with dimensions of 3, 4, and 5 holes long on the sides. The angle opposite the 4-hole-long side is 53.13 degrees, which matches the angle of a bent liftarm. Since the triangle's angle and the bent liftarm angle are the same, bent liftarms can now be added onto the triangle, and LEGO hole spacing will be maintained for the rest of the structure. Continuing on with the building steps following Figure 3-11 shows how this works.

Figure 3-11. *A triangle results from step 4*

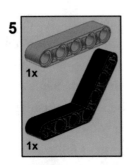

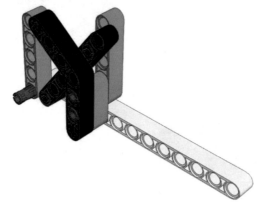

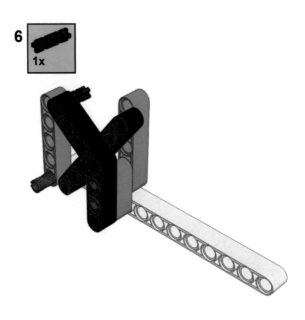

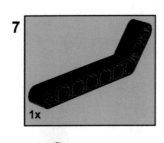

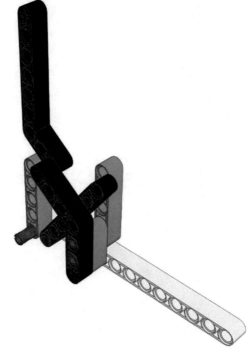

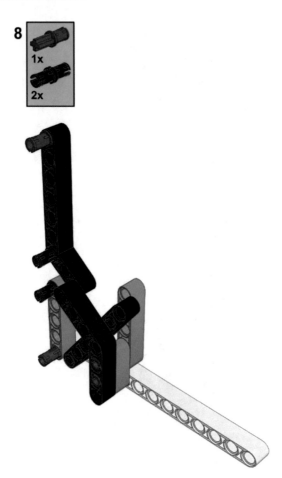

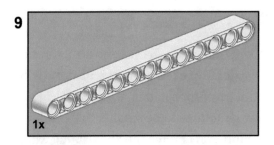

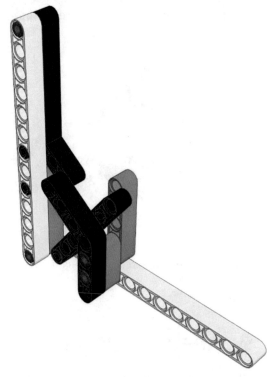

Pushing on one of the long sides of the Triangle Trick will show that the structure is rather strong—it doesn't bend much. This is because the triangles built into the design are effective at distributing a load. So when strength is needed in a LEGO design, a triangular load-bearing shape is a good idea. The 53.13 angle of bent liftarms allows incorporation of these triangles.

Connectors

This chapter has shown that many shapes and structures can be built out of liftarms, pins, and axles. But even more can be done with connectors that come in the Robot Inventor set, diagrammed in Figure 3-12. Connectors can allow structures to be smaller than building with only liftarms. Also, connectors can change the angle along which things are build, allowing large three-dimensional structures. Connectors can include both pin and axle openings.

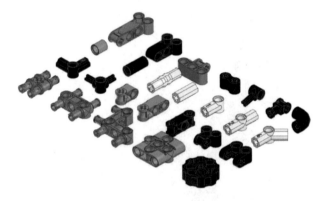

Figure 3-12.   *The Robot Inventor set includes many types of connectors*

Exercise: Symmetric Objects

An interesting challenge in building with LEGO is to make three-dimensional shapes that are symmetrical. Symmetry means that if an imaginary line were drawn down the middle of a side, then the two halves of the side are mirror images of each other. Figure 3-13 shows two examples of structures that have three-dimensional symmetry. For each side viewed, there's a mirror image at the line down the middle of the side. Building these two examples starts with building instructions following Figure 3-13 to first build the Symmetric Cube.

Figure 3-13. *The Symmetric Cube (at left) and Symmetric Cross (at right) are built with connectors*

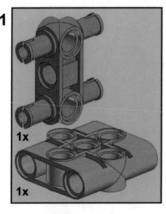

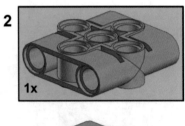

The Symmetric Cube shows the idea of symmetry, as diagrammed in Figure 3-14. If an imaginary line were drawn down the center of a side of the cube's face, the left and right halves are mirror images of each other. This symmetry will be the case no matter what side of the Symmetric Cube is being viewed.

Two halves are mirror images of each other.

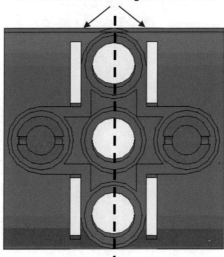

Figure 3-14. *All the sides of the Symmetric Cube show symmetry about a horizontal or vertical line*

The Symmetric Cube is a simple design, but a more complex example can be studied with the Symmetric Cross as follows:

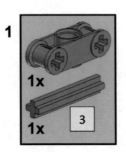

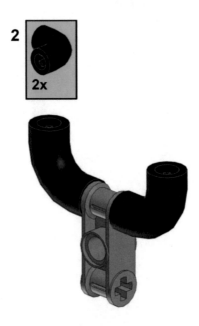

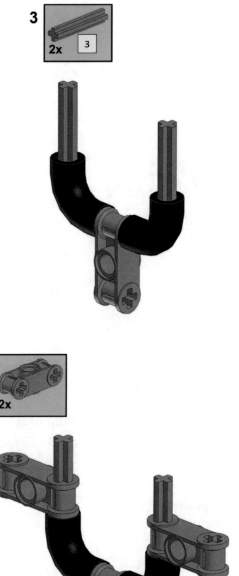

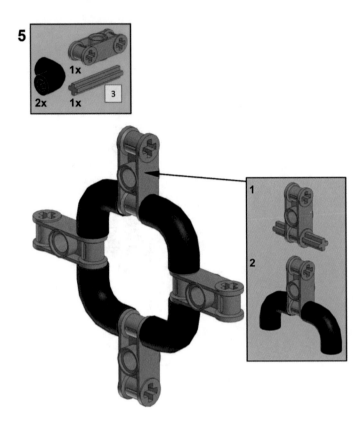

For an even more extensive study of symmetry, the Symmetric Cube and the Symmetric Cross can be combined as in Figure 3-15 to build the Symmetric Star. Directions to build the Symmetric Star follow Figure 3-15. The Symmetric Cube goes into the center of the Symmetric Cross, held in place with connectors and pins.

Figure 3-15. *The Symmetric Star incorporates both the Symmetric Cube and the Symmetric Cross*

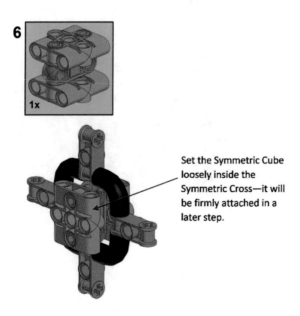

Set the Symmetric Cube loosely inside the Symmetric Cross—it will be firmly attached in a later step.

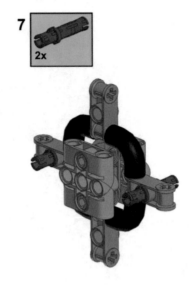

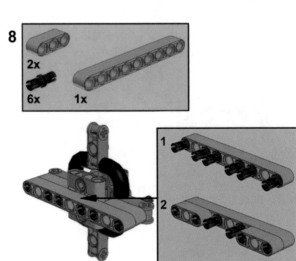

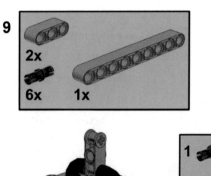

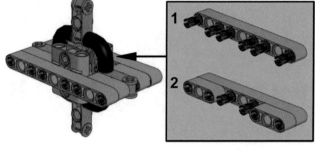

Project: Mechanical Linkages

This chapter has given a tour of the building elements that come with the Robot Inventor and SPIKE Prime sets: liftarms, pins, axles, bushes, and connectors. Exercises have built several structures to see how all these building elements can be used together. But aside from structures, parts that move can also be built, called linkages. A mechanical *linkage* is an assembly of building elements to control movement. Two example linkages are built as follows: a universal joint and an eccentric.

The Universal Joint

The Universal Joint, shown in Figure 3-16, allows an axle to spin in an arrangement where the axle isn't in a straight line. This can be useful for a situation in which one part of a shaft needs to flex, such as with cars and trucks that have wheels bounce up and down as the vehicle drives. A pivoting mechanism allows the entire length of the axle to spin, even though there is an angle between two sections of the axle. Connectors are used in the following LEGO example to create a pivoting action that accommodates the angle between the two axle sections. When one end of the axle spun, such as by the handle on the right side of the Universal Joint, the entire length of the axle will rotate. The angle between the two sections of the Universal Joint can be changed and still be able to rotate the axle.

Figure 3-16. *A universal joint allows an axle to spin when there is an angular bend in the axle*

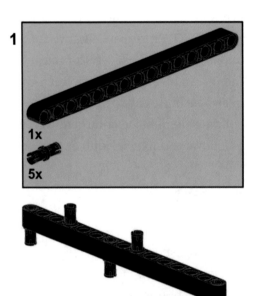

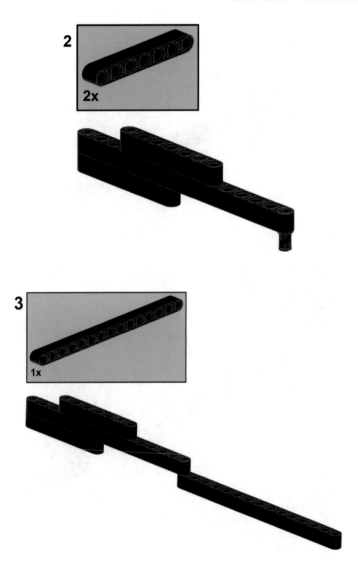

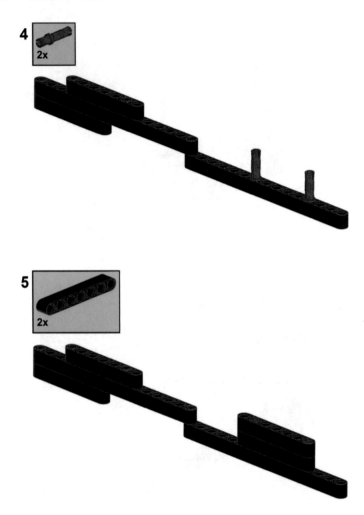

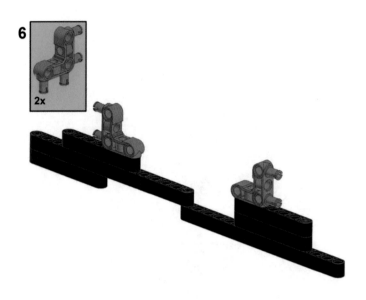

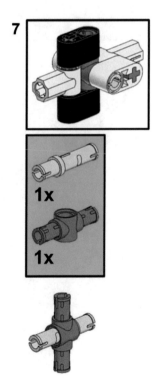

8

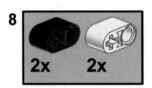

9

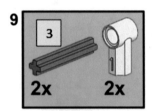

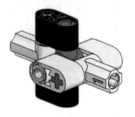

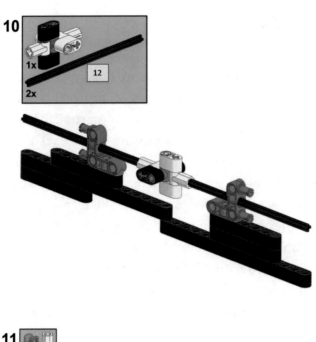

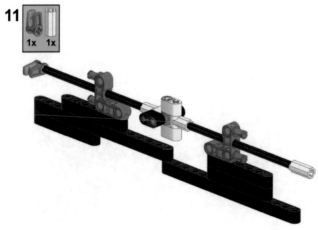

The Eccentric

One problem that often comes up when designing machinery is how
to change rotary motion into linear motion. *Rotary motion* is spinning
motion, commonly encountered from a motor, engine, or manual crank
handle. In contrast, *linear motion* moves along a straight line that might
be wanted to use to push something forward or in a back-and-forth action.
A linkage known as an *eccentric* solves the problem of converting rotary
motion to linear motion by attaching a part called a link to a rotating circle.
As a result, the link converts the rotary movement created by turning
the crank into the linear movement of the axle: the axle slides back and
forth as the crank is turned. Figure 3-17 shows a LEGO implementation
of an eccentric, with building instructions following the figure. Turning
the crank handle results in the axle sliding back and forth along a line.
A version of this eccentric will be used in a more advanced project in
Chapter 9.

Figure 3-17. *The eccentric converts rotary motion into linear motion*

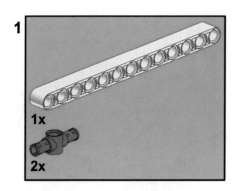

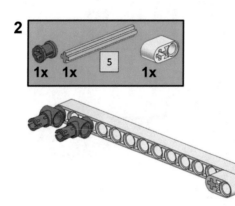

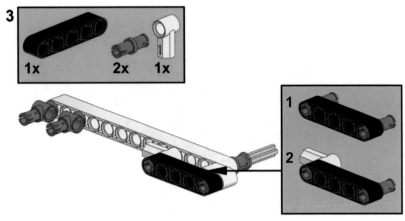

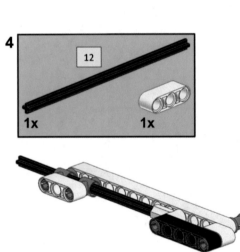

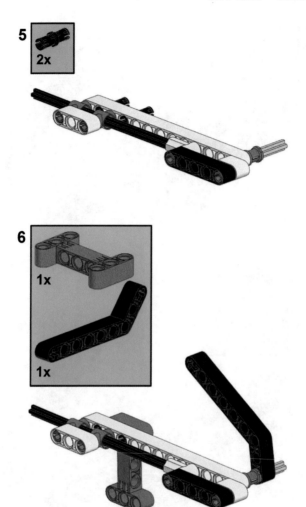

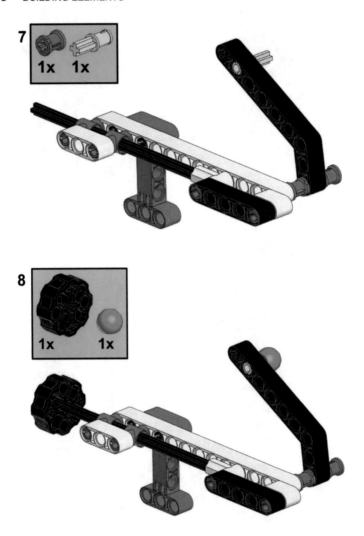

Summary

This chapter gave a tour of the building elements of the Robot Inventor set including liftarms, pins, axles, bushes, and connectors. Liftarms are the fundamental building element in the Robot Inventor and SPIKE Prime sets and come in shapes of straight, bent, rectangular, and letters of the alphabet. Example projects showed how these various liftarm shapes can be used, such as the angle of bent liftarms allowing triangular supports to make structures strong. Liftarms include attachment holes for either pins or axles so that liftarms can be joined together. Pins are inserted into the circular openings of liftarms, while axles are inserted into cross-shaped openings. Some pins have an axle on one end for conversion from pin connection to axle connection. Pins can also be with or without friction ridges to allow choice in whether a connection between liftarms should be resistant to or freely allowed to rotate. The many varieties of connectors that come with the Robot Inventor set are another means to join liftarms, offering more design flexibility than the simpler approach of pins and axles. While building elements are often used to build nonmoving structures, building elements can also be used to build machines with moving parts, as demonstrated with the example linkages built in the chapter summary projects.

CHAPTER 4

Gears

Most power sources, like motors or engines, provide power to a device by rotating a shaft. But, from there, this rotation often needs to be transformed into some other kind of motion. For example, there may be a need to change the speed of the rotation of a LEGO motor. Or perhaps the need is to change the direction of the rotation or make the motor push harder than it currently does. Gears allow all these transformations. This chapter starts with a tour of the gears that come in the Robot Inventor set. After that, a series of exercises teaches how to increase or decrease the speed of rotation with techniques called gearing up and gearing down, how a force called torque affects the ability to speed up a gear system, and how to build a system with multiple gear pairings. This chapter's project is to build a device called a transmission that allows a switch back and forth from a low-speed to a high-speed gear configuration.

Gears in the Robot Inventor Set

Gears are parts whose teeth mesh with each other as they rotate, and they're often named based on how many teeth they have. Table 4-1 lists the many gears included in the Robot Inventor set, including the number of teeth for each gear. Figure 4-1 shows what these gears look like.

© Grady Koch 2023
G. Koch, *Learn Engineering with LEGO*, Maker Innovations Series,
https://doi.org/10.1007/978-1-4842-9280-8_4

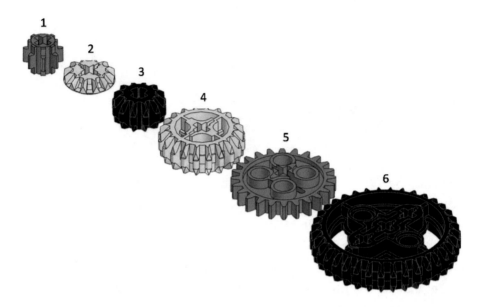

Figure 4-1. *The Robot Inventor set includes six varieties of gears*

Table 4-1. *Gears in the Robot Inventor Set*

Figure 4-1 Label #	Gear Type	Number of Teeth	Quantity in Set	Part Number
1	Spur	8	2	10928
2	Single bevel	12	5	6589
3	Double bevel	12	4	32270
4	Double bevel	20	4	32269
5	Spur	24	2	3648
6	Double bevel	36	1	32498

Aside from the number of teeth, gears differ in shape, giving rise to three types: spur, single bevel, and double bevel.

Spur Gears

Spur gears (#1 and #5 in Figure 4-1) are meant to be meshed together in a straight line, such as in Figure 4-2. Spur gears are usually used with other spur gears. Meshing a spur gear with either a single-bevel or double-bevel gear doesn't work, since they won't be spaced at a proper distance to fit along a straight line of LEGO holes. Though not common, there are ways of using bent liftarms to combine spur gears with beveled gears, described in the following sidebar.

Figure 4-2. *Spur gears mesh with each other in a side-by-side arrangement*

MESHING SPUR GEARS WITH LIFTARMS

Meshing a spur gear with a double-bevel gear in a straight liftarm doesn't work, since the spacing in the liftarm's holes doesn't match the gears' diameters. However, it does work to mesh a spur gear with a double-bevel gear using a bent liftarm, as shown in Figure 4-3.

Figure 4-3. *Spur and bevel gears can be meshed by using bent liftarms*

Beveled Gears

A *bevel* is an angle cut in the edge of a surface, which rounds off sharp corners. Looking closely at the teeth of a beveled gear, such as in Figure 4-4, will show that the edges of the teeth are cut at an angle. Spur gears, on the other hand, don't have this angle on the teeth edges. Bevels are used on gears so that they can be oriented perpendicular to each other with the teeth meshing together, such as in Figure 4-5. This sideways turn comes in useful in changing the plane of rotation, which will be employed in the Many-Geared Machine exercise later in this chapter and the Mechanized Cannon of Chapter 5.

Figure 4-4. *Beveled gears have the edges of their teeth cut off at an angle*

Figure 4-5. *Beveled gears can mesh against each other in a perpendicular arrangement*

Robot Inventor comes with two types of beveled gears: the single bevel (#2 in Figure 4-1) and double bevel (#3, #4, and #6 in Figure 4-1). The *single-bevel gear*, which comes in only one size, has teeth on one side, but not the other. This arrangement makes the gear thin enough to fit into small spaces. For example, in Chapter 5, five single-bevel gears will be combined in a small housing to build a mechanism known as a differential. This use in a differential is also why Robot Inventor comes with so many single-bevel gears. It should be noted that single-bevel gears are not meant to mesh with each other (or with double-bevel gears) in a straight line, like spur gears, but rather in a perpendicular arrangement.

Double-bevel gears have beveled teeth on both sides. This arrangement can be thought of as two single-bevel gears joined together on their flat faces. The advantage of double-bevel gears is that they can be used in either straight lines (like a spur gear) or in a perpendicular arrangement. The disadvantage of double-bevel gears is that they're thick and may not fit into some inventions.

Speeding Up Rotation, or "Gearing Up"

The Speed Increaser shown in Figure 4-6 is a good introduction to working with gears. Building instructions follow the figure. The pair of gears involved in this design will increase the speed of rotation from the motor, called *gearing up*.

Figure 4-6. *The Speed Increaser uses a pair of gears to increase the speed of rotation from a motor*

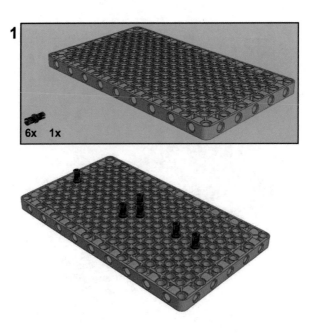

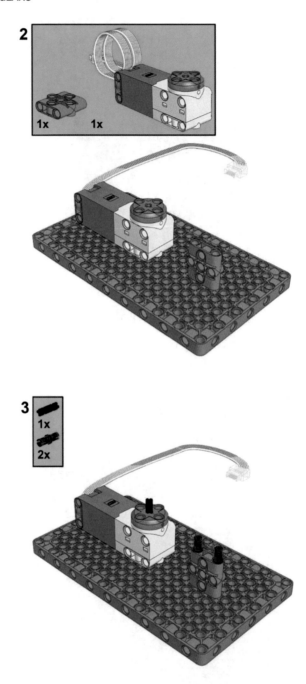

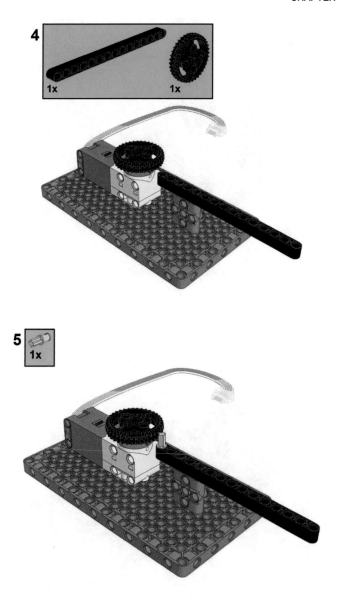

6

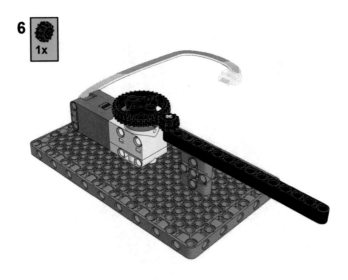

7

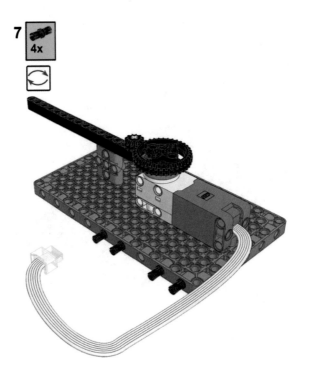

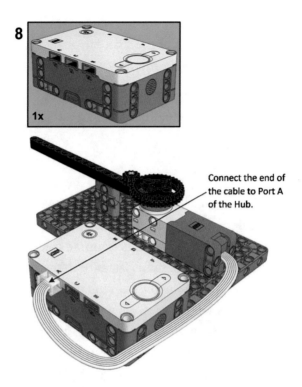

Connect the end of
the cable to Port A
of the Hub.

The Speed Increaser can be activated by using the front panel of the
Hub to turn on the motor, as described in Chapter 1. As the motor spins
the 36-tooth gear, the 12-tooth gear spins in the opposite direction, which
shows an important feature of gears that adjacent gears have opposite
directions of rotation. So, for example, if one gear is going clockwise, then
the gear next to it will go counterclockwise.

The gears also spin at different speeds, with the 12-tooth gear spinning
faster than the 36-tooth gear, leading to the name of this design as gearing
up. The 36-tooth gear is providing motion to the gear pair, so it is called a
driver gear. Since the 12-tooth gear follows the motion of the driver gear,
the 12-tooth gear is called a *follower gear*. Counting the rotations of each
of the two gears, which should be easier to do at a low-speed setting on

the motor, should reveal that the 12-tooth gear rotates in a complete circle three times for every one rotation of the 36-tooth gear. This increase in speed can be calculated by the *gear ratio*:

$$\text{gear ratio} = \text{number of teeth on follower gear} / \text{number of teeth on driver gear}$$

$$= 12/36$$

$$= 1/3$$

A way to visualize the effect of the gear ratio on speed is to consider the fraction, with the denominator of the fraction as the relative speed of the second gear. So the 1/3 result of this example calculation means that the follower gear will go three times faster than the driver gear. If the denominator of the fraction gets larger than the numerator, the follower gear will go faster. In other words, a lower gear ratio means faster speed.

Gearing up can be useful in designs to spin an axle at a faster speed than a motor can provide. When a motor is at its highest speed setting, and the need is to spin faster, a pair of gears can get the higher-speed rotation. And by changing the size of one or both of the gears, the gear ratio can be tailored to adjust speed.

Slowing Down Rotation, or "Gearing Down"

The Speed Increaser showed how to increase the speed of rotation from a motor, but a gear pair can also be used to slow down rotation. This slowing down can be done by reversing the order of the gears to have a small driver gear drive a large follower gear, as in Figure 4-7. To build this design, the gears on the Speed Increaser can simply be reversed in order. As the motor is activated, the follower gear spins at a slower speed than the driver gear.

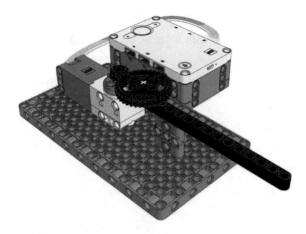

Figure 4-7. *Gearing down involves a small driver gear and a large follower gear*

This reduction in speed, which occurs when using a small driver gear and large follower gear, is known as *gearing down*. With the motor speed at a slow rate, counting gear rotations should show that the 12-tooth driver gear has to spin around three times to get the 36-tooth gear to spin around once. A calculation of the gear ratio will also indicate the reduction in speed:

> gear ratio = number of teeth on follower gear /
> number of teeth on driver gear
>
> = 36/12
>
> = 3/1

Exercise: The Many-Geared Machine

The gearing up and gearing down exercise of the previous sections used a single pair of gears, but sometimes a design may need to use more than one pair of gears. Such a need for multiple gear pairs may come up to have more flexibility in getting a particular gear ratio, to change the

direction of rotation, or span a long distance between a motor and wheel.
Aside from these practical applications, it's also interesting to watch the
spinning of many gears all meshed together. So to explore the use and
fun of multiple gear pairs, Figure 4-8 presents the Many-Geared Machine.
The construction builds on the preceding gearing up and gearing down
exercise, so the first step for the Many-Geared Machine begins at number
9. The Many-Geared Machine features gears meshed at a right angle, in
addition to being in a straight line.

Figure 4-8. *The Many-Geared Machine uses all three types of gears in
the Robot Inventor set: spur, single bevel, and double bevel*

9

Notice that the order of gears is in the gearing down configuration.

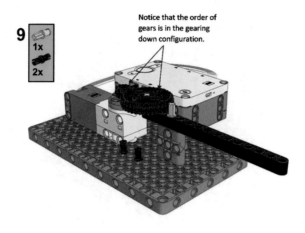

10

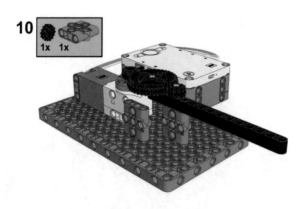

11

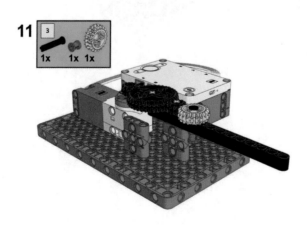

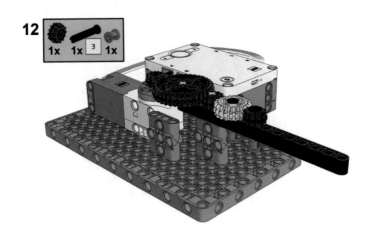

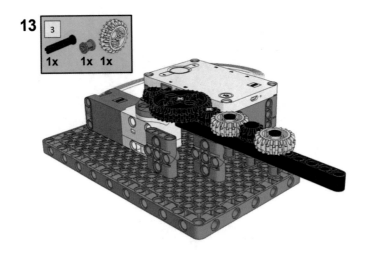

14

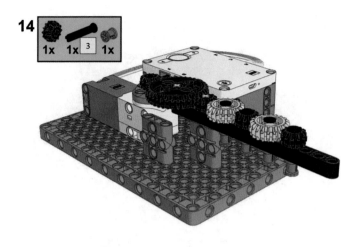

15

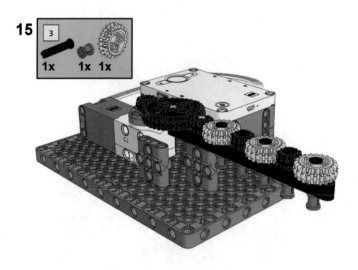

16

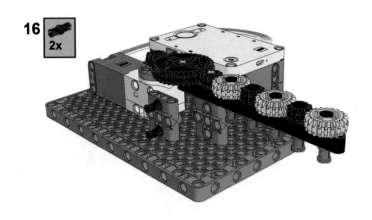

17

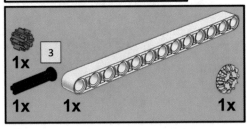

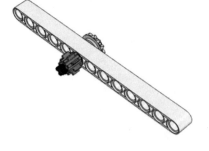

18

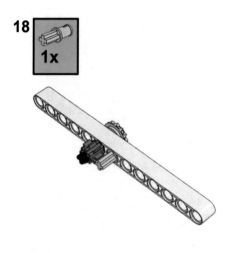

19

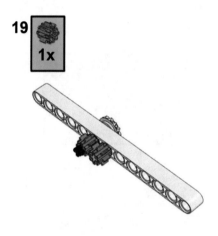

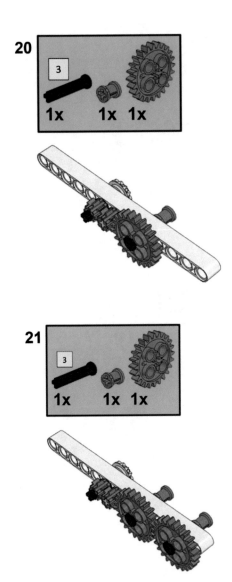

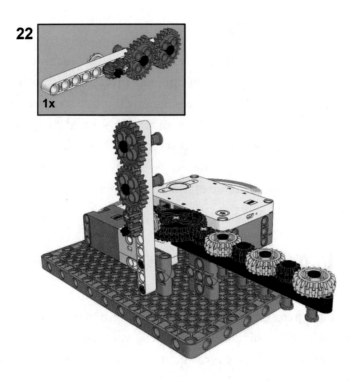

Turning on the Many-Geared Machine, using the Hub to control the motor as described in Chapter 1, demonstrates several properties of gear systems:

- Some gears spin faster than others.

- Adjacent gears spin in opposite directions.

- Gears can be meshed perpendicularly, as well as in a straight line.

These effects will be explored in detail in the following two sections.

Direction of Rotation

Studying all the gears in motion of the Many-Geared Machine shows that gears adjacent to each other spin in opposite directions. If a driver gear is rotating clockwise, then the follower gear will rotate counterclockwise. Sometimes, a design requirement in a machine is that the rotation of the output shaft must have a particular direction. If a gear design rotates in the wrong direction, adding one more gear will convert rotation to the needed direction. This extra gear can be of the same size as the final gear, in case the gear ratio needs to stay the same.

Calculating Gear Ratio for More Than Two Gears

An earlier section in this chapter described how to calculate the gear ratio for a single pair of gears: the number of teeth of the follower gear divided by the number of teeth on the driver gear. When more than one pair of gears is involved, the overall gear ratio is found by multiplying the gear ratios of each pair that makes up the gear system. As each gear pair is analyzed, the calculation is made easier by keeping in mind that each follower gear (save the last) is the driver of the next gear pair. For example, in the straight-line section of the Many-Geared Machine of Figure 4-8, although there are eight gears, there are only seven pairs of gears: the first and second gears are one pair, the second gear and the third are another, and so on. Table 4-2 walks through an example calculation for the straight-line section of the Many-Geared Machine.

Table 4-2. *Calculation of the Gear Ratio for the Straight-Line Section of the Many-Geared Machine*

Gear Pair	Driver Gear Size (Number of Teeth)	Follower Gear Size (Number of Teeth)	Pair Gear Ratio
1–2	12	36	3
2–3	36	12	0.33
3–4	12	20	1.67
4–5	20	12	0.60
5–6	12	20	1.67
6–7	20	12	0.60
7–8	12	20	1.67
System gear ratio (multiply together all seven pair gear ratios)			1.67

In this case, the result of the system gear ratio calculation is 1.67. There's actually a shortcut to calculating the gear ratio for multiple gear pairs that are all lined up in a row, as in this example. The shortcut is to just consider the last gear in the line and the first gear in the line. In this exercise, this calculation would be 20/12 = 1.67. However, this shortcut doesn't work for the more complex example of compound gear in a following exercise.

Recalling that the speed factor is the inverse of the gear ratio, the calculated gear ratio of 1.67 means that the speed of the last gear is 1/1.67 = 0.6 times the first gear. So this gear system is a speed reducer. A simple rule to remember: To decrease speed, the gear ratio has to be greater than 1. A gear ratio of less than 1 will be a speed increaser.

One reason to use multiple gear pairs is to customize a gear ratio to an exact value desired. Many more gear ratios can be achieved by combining gear pairs of various sizes, rather than just combining two gears for a single pair.

The Many-Geared Machine also has a perpendicular line of gears that begins with 12-tooth and 36-tooth gears attached parallel to the base plate. The line of gears then bends at a right angle, with a 12-tooth single-bevel gear making the turn. The total gear ratio for the perpendicular line of gears can also be calculated by multiplying the gear ratios of each pair of gears. However, the perpendicular line of gears has an extra feature called a compound gear that makes the calculation a little more complicated. Compound gears are a subject presented later in this chapter. But before getting into compound gears, the subject of torque should be understood.

Exercise: The Torque Demonstrator

Torque is the amount of force involved in rotation, such as in the rotation of gears. A motor or hand crank supplies torque to a gear system to get the gears rotating; this, in turn, supplies the rotational force to power some desired motion, like spinning the wheels of a vehicle. Torque doesn't really come into play in the previous examples of the Speed Increaser and the Many-Geared Machine, because the gears aren't doing any work; they're not pushing against anything except each other. But in practical use, gears serve a purpose to move something else, like the wheels of a robot or vehicle.

Torque can be experienced by building the Torque Demonstrator shown in Figure 4-9 and built with the directions following the figure. The motor is not plugged into anything in the Torque Demonstrator. Instead, the motor is used here to provide resistance to motion.

Figure 4-9. *Resistance will be felt in turning the crank of the Torque Demonstrator*

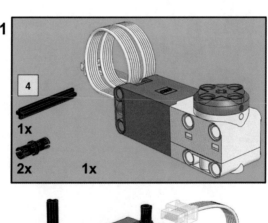

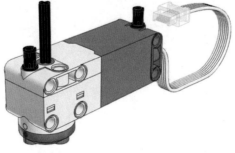

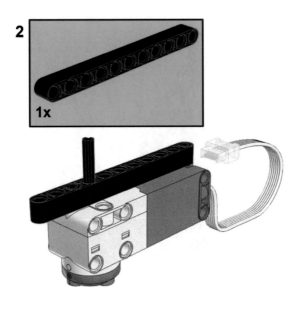

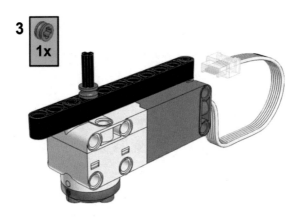

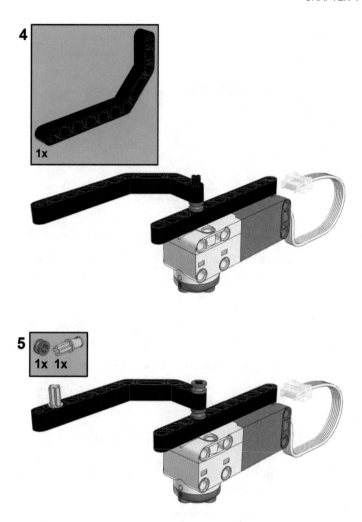

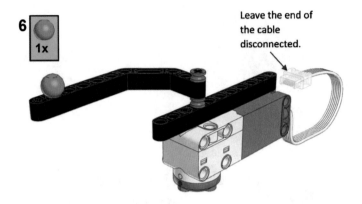

As the crank handle of the Torque Demonstrator is rotated, resistance should be felt. Torque is required, in this case by the force applied on the crank, to overcome the resistance to motion presented by the motor. And the faster the crank, the more torque is needed. The Torque Demonstrator shouldn't be used too much, or cranked too hard, since it's possible with excessive force to damage the motor. For now, the Torque Demonstrator should be set aside to compare with the next exercise in manipulating torque.

Lowering Torque by Gearing Down

A key advantage of gear designs is that they can control the torque required to get a machine in motion. This useful effect can be tested by building another version of the Torque Demonstrator, called the Torque Reducer, shown in Figure 4-10. The Torque Reducer is similar to the Torque Demonstrator, except that it includes a gear system. In setting out to build the Torque Reducer, the Torque Demonstrator built in the previous section should be set aside so performance between the two devices can be compared.

Figure 4-10. *The Torque Reducer uses a pair of gears to reduce the torque required to turn the crank*

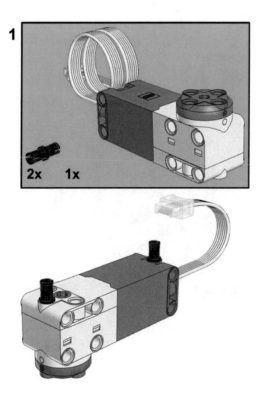

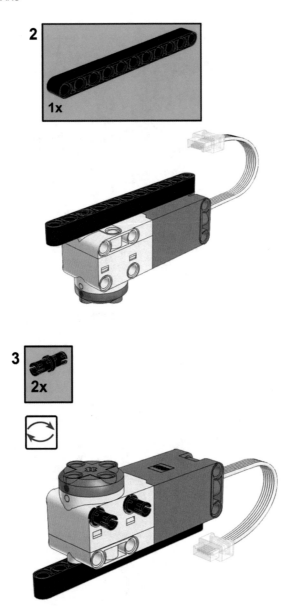

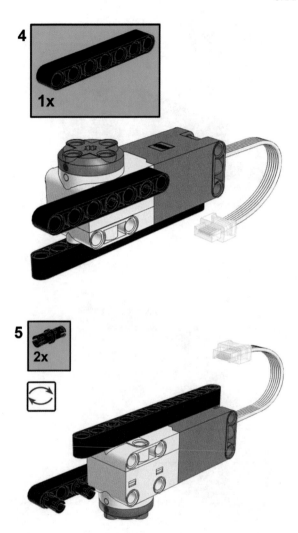

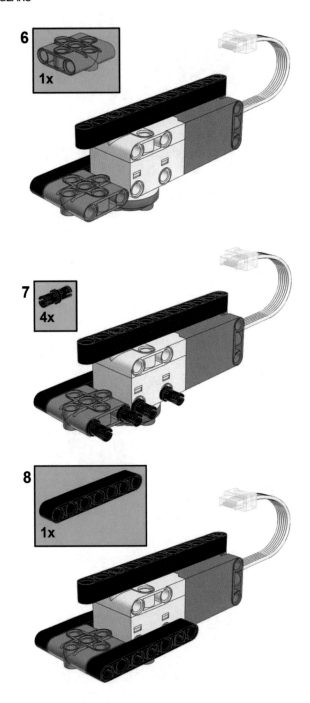

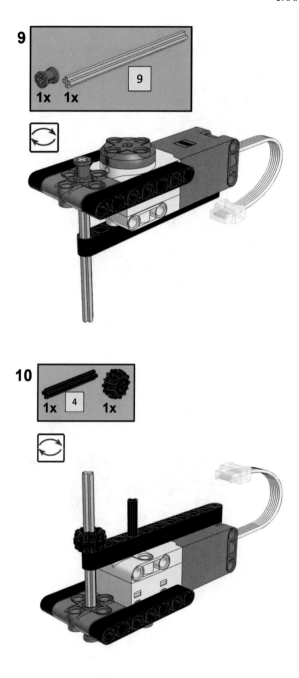

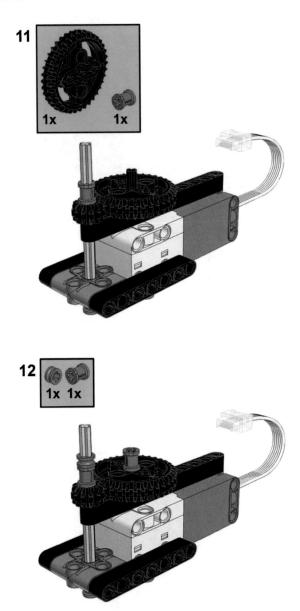

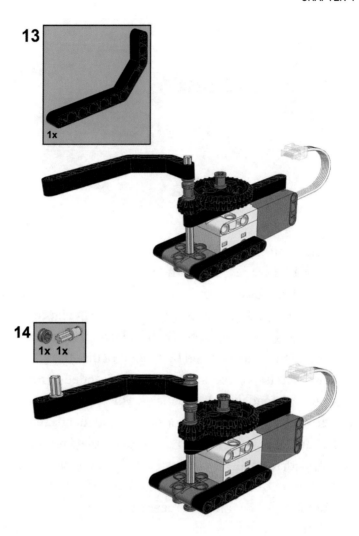

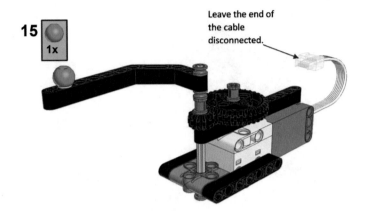

15 1x

Leave the end of
the cable
disconnected.

Rotating the hand crank on the Torque Reducer requires less force than needed for the Torque Demonstrator. This is because the pair of gears has reduced the torque required to push against the resistance of the motor. The gear pairing is the same as the one used in Figure 4-7 for the exercise on changing rotation speed. As calculated in that exercise, this gearing down design reduces speed by a factor of three.

Now in this exercise, by reducing the torque needed to rotate the crank, the system's speed was also reduced. This is an important principle of gear design: reducing the level of torque needed means reducing speed. On the other hand, a lower gear ratio to increase speed requires that higher torque be supplied; this will be explored in the next section. A gear ratio also indicates the factor of reducing required torque—in this example of the Torque Reducer, the gear pair reduces the needed torque by a factor of three over the Torque Demonstrator.

Raising Speed by Attempting to Raise Input Torque (and Failing)

A scenario could be imagined where higher speed is desired for the Torque Demonstrator of Figure 4-9. Experimenting with the Torque Reducer showed that it's possible to reduce input torque at the expense of a lower speed.

But perhaps there's a situation where lots of input torque are available to hopefully get higher speed. Experiments with gearing up in an earlier section showed that if the gear order of the Torque Reducer were reversed, then the speed would increase by a factor of three. In other words, the Torque Reducer would become the Speed Increaser. Testing this idea is just a simple matter of reversing the gears in the Torque Reducer to look like Figure 4-11.

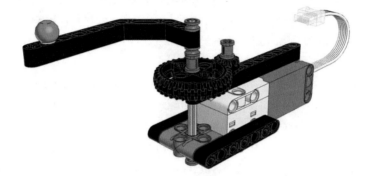

Figure 4-11. *Reversing the gears of the Torque Reducer (Figure 4-10) could theoretically give a higher rotation speed, but it doesn't work in practice*

But trying to turn this crank on the Speed Increaser will show that this design doesn't work: the resistance to motion is too strong. The torque required to turn the crank is so high that the LEGO parts can't handle the load. The gears may even start to slip against each other. This design is a failure, as there is no way to reliably get the machine moving.

This failure provides an example of the trade-off between torque and speed in gear systems. The idea with the Speed Increaser was to achieve a high speed of rotation, but the required input torque couldn't be supplied. The higher the speed of rotation in a gear design, the higher the torque it needs. In other words, increasing speed is limited by the availability of input torque. However, there is a way to help increase speed when available torque is limited: using a device called a transmission, built in the closing project of this chapter.

Exercise: The Compound-Gear Spinner

The previous sections described how the gear ratio affects speed and torque and that a specific gear ratio may be required. Using the simple arrangement of gear pairs in series—that is, lined up along the same line—makes it difficult to get a low gear ratio for high speed. This is because to gear up with a first pair of gears, a small follower gear has to be used. This small follower then becomes a small driver gear, likely forcing the creation of a gearing down gear pair. These gearing up and gearing down pairs tend to then cancel each other out.

A way around this problem, when a low gear ratio is desired, is to use a design known as compound gears. This involves putting two gears parallel to each other on the same axle, allowing their gear pair ratios to be independent of each other. Figure 4-12 shows the use of such a design in the Compound-Gear Spinner, which can be built with the instructions that follow the figure.

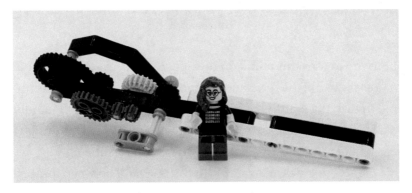

Figure 4-12. *The Compound-Gear Spinner provides a high gear ratio to create a fast rotation of the yellow output axle*

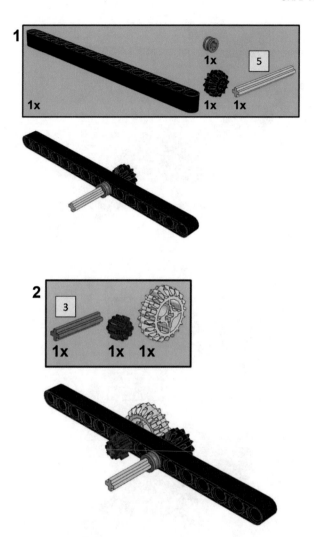

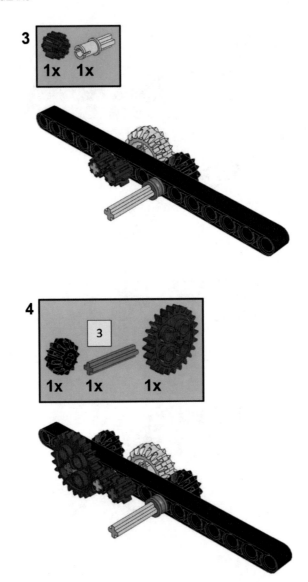

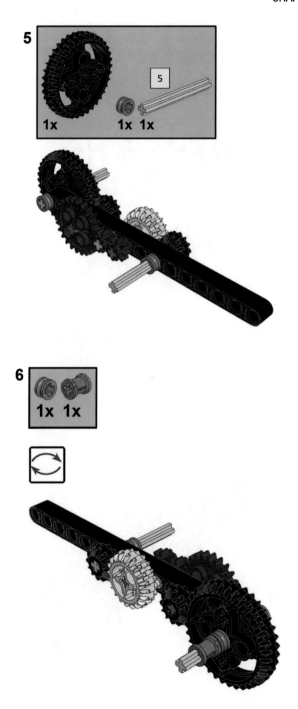

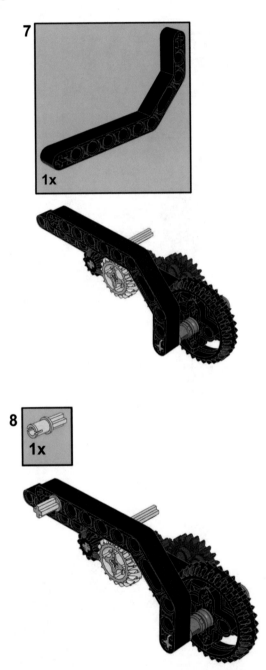

11

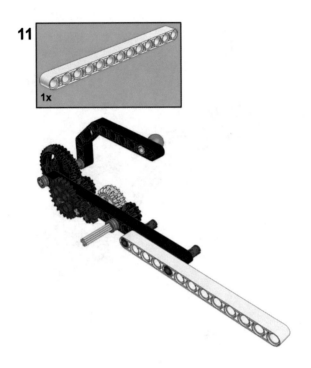

12

13

14

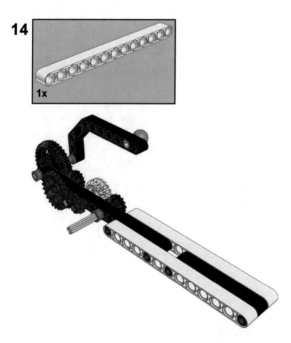

Turning the crank handle on the Compound-Gear Spinner should show that the gray connector on the output axle spins quite fast. To figure out how fast, the total gear ratio can be calculated by considering the four pairs of gears involved in the design. Table 4-3 summarizes this calculation, which considers the first gear to be the 36-tooth double-bevel gear connected to the crank handle.

Table 4-3. *There Are Four Gear Pairs in the Compound-Gear Spinner*

Gear Pair (in Figure 4-12)	Driver Gear Size (Number of Teeth)	Follower Gear Size (Number of Teeth)	Pair Gear Ratio
1–2	36	12	0.33
3–4	24	8	0.33
4–5	8	8	1
6–7	20	12	0.60
System gear ratio (multiply together all four pair gear ratios)			**0.065**

The gear ratio calculation produces a result of 0.065, suggesting that the speed of the output should be large for such a small gear ratio. The speed multiplication is the inverse of the gear ratio, meaning that the gray connector on the output shaft spins $1/0.065 = 15$ times for every single rotation of the input crank handle.

This high-speed rotation works in this case because the Compound-Gear Spinner is moving only a lightweight gray connector on the output shaft, so the needed input torque from hand cranking the input handle is manageable. But something a little heavier on the output axle, like the bent liftarm in Figure 4-13, should reveal that more torque is needed on the crank handle. The design still works with this slightly heavier load, but the torque involved approaches the limit of what the Compound-Gear Spinner can handle. If such a low gear ratio were tried to power the wheels of a robot, then it would be unlikely that enough torque could be supplied to get the robot moving.

Figure 4-13. *Increasing the weight of the load by replacing the gray connector with a bent liftarm requires higher input torque on the crank handle*

Project: Two-Speed Transmission

This chapter has shown several examples of how designing gear systems involves making trade-offs between speed and torque. For a high speed, higher torque must be available. If available torque is limited, then a design will have to settle for a lower speed. So it would be desirable for a device that can allow a rapid shift between a low-torque, low-speed setup and a high-torque, high-speed one. For example, when a car is at a standstill, a low-torque, low-speed gear system would be good to get the car moving. Then when the car is moving, a switchover to a high-torque, high-speed gear system could help the car speed up.

Fortunately, such devices exist, called a transmission. A *transmission* allows switching between gear systems so that the speed and torque relationship can be optimized. Transmissions are commonly found in everyday life in cars and trucks, though nowadays gear switching is often automatic, so not much attention is paid to gear switching. A LEGO version of a transmission is shown in Figure 4-14, which is called the Two-Speed Transmission. This project allows the selection of two different speed settings: the load of four wheels can move slowly (with low torque required) or fast (with high torque required). The set of four wheels is used here to give some weight on the output axle so that the torque involved can be felt as the spin handle is turned.

gear shifter: push in for high speed, pull out for low speed

spin handle

Figure 4-14. *The Two-Speed Transmission offers a selection of high-speed or low-speed gear settings*

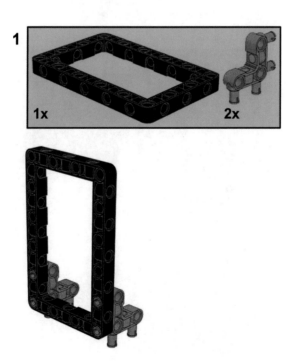

2

3

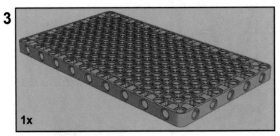

4

5

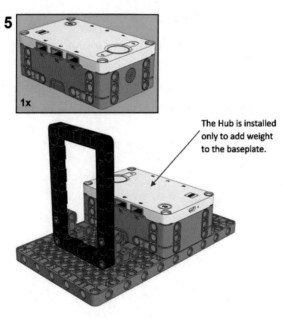

The Hub is installed
only to add weight
to the baseplate.

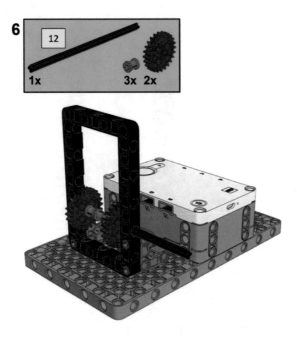

Steps 6–8 can be difficult in the installation of axles with gears on them. Figure 4-15 gives a suggestion to push the axle partially through one side of the liftarm. Gears and bushing can then be placed, pushing the axle through each gear or bushing after it has been attached.

Figure 4-15. *Assembly technique for steps 6–8*

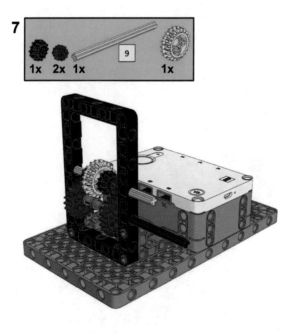

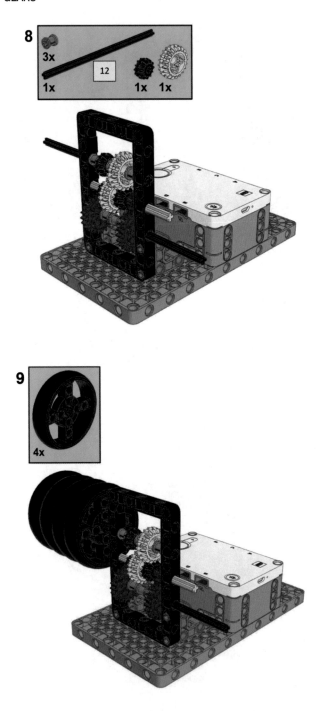

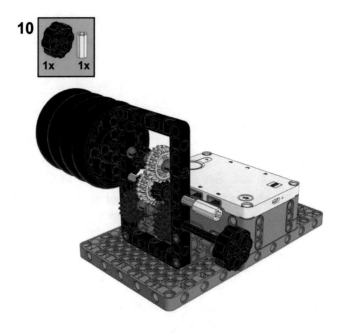

Turning the spin handle on the transmission results in rotation of the wheels on the output axis. Experimenting with the gear shifter will show that on the low-speed setting, the wheels are easier to get moving than on the high-speed setting. So if the transmission was driving the wheels of a car, it would be easier to get the car moving from a standstill using the low-speed setting on the transmission. Then once moving, to get a high speed from the wheels, a shift should be made to the high-speed gear selection. The speeds allowed by each of the two gear choices can be determined from the gear ratios. Calculating the gear ratio is a matter of multiplying the ratios of the gear pairs of the transmission, such as the calculation in Table 4-4. The first gear in this calculation is the 24-tooth spur gear on the same axle as the spin handle, which meshes with an 8-tooth spur gear for a gear ratio of 0.33. This first gear ratio then gets multiplied by the gear ratio chosen by the gear shifter, which can either be a 20-tooth gear driving a

12-tooth gear or a 12-tooth gear driving a 20-tooth gear. The end result is that the wheels on the output axle can be rotating at either 5 or 1.8 times the speed of the input spin handle, depending on the gear pair selected by the gear shifter.

Table 4-4. *There Are Two Options for the Gear Ratio of the Two-Speed Transmission*

Gear Pair (in Figure 4-15)	Driver Gear Size (Number of Teeth)	Follower Gear Size (Number of Teeth)	Pair Gear Ratio
1–2	24	8	0.33
3–4 (high-speed setting)	20	12	0.60
3–4 (low-speed setting)	12	20	1.67
System gear ratio (multiply pair 1–2 by either choice of pair 3–4)			0.20 or 0.55

Summary

This chapter described how to use gears to transform rotational power to change speed, torque, or direction of rotation. These techniques are rather useful since most power sources, such as engines and motors, provide power in the form of rotation. There are three different types of gears in the Robot Inventor set, including spur gears, single-bevel gears, and double-bevel gears. Spur gears are meant to mesh with each other in a straight line, while beveled gears can be meshed against each other in a right angle. Double-bevel gears have the ability to mesh in either straight line or right angles, but at the disadvantage of being thick and bulky. Much of the function of a system of gears can be described by the gear ratio, which indicates change in speed that gears produce. Exercises showed gear designs to either decrease the gear ratio (called gearing up) or increase the gear ratio (called gearing down). With a lower gear ratio, an axle can be made to spin faster. However, spinning faster with a low gear ratio involves a trade-off with the amount of force, called torque, required to get the gear system moving. Speed and torque are related to each other, with high speed from a gear system coming at the expense of needing a high input torque. In some designs, the torque required to get a high gear ratio moving is so high that the mechanical system can't handle the torque needed. Instead of using a single pair of gears, multiple pairs of gears can be combined to customize a gear ratio, change the direction of rotation, or reach to an axle that is farther away. In the case of multiple gears, the overall gear ratio is calculated by multiplying the gear ratios for each gear pair in the system of gears. Multiple gear pairs all lined up can give flexibility in tailoring a gear design, but can't get to a low gear ratio because the gearing up of one pair of gears usually involves gearing down for the next gear pair. A way to get around the problem of gears all lined up is to use compound gears, where two gears are combined onto a single axle. It can be advantageous to switch gear ratios in a machine, such as a wheeled vehicle, which can be accomplished with a transmission.

## CHAPTER 5

Mechanisms

A *mechanism* is a system of mechanical parts working together in a machine to create a desired action. Such a desired action could be to lift, spin, push, nudge, drive, or shoot. This chapter presents four example mechanisms to build: a ratchet, cam, differential, and turntable. These mechanisms are commonly used in designing robots and vehicles, so an understanding of these mechanisms serves well in creating custom designs. A variety of parts will be used from the Robot Inventor to build these example mechanisms, including the building elements and gears of the previous two chapters. There are also several components in the Robot Inventor set that are meant specifically for use in particular mechanisms, including turntables, differential, and dart shooter. The final project in this chapter combines several mechanisms to build a steerable cannon.

Exercise: The Ratchet

A *ratchet* is a mechanism that allows an axle or wheel to rotate in one direction (say clockwise), but blocks rotation in the other direction (counterclockwise). In daily life, ratchets can be seen at turnstiles where people are allowed to move forward through a gate, but not backward, such as at a train station, amusement part, or places that scan a ticket for entry. Also, a ratchet wrench for tightening or loosening bolts is a common tool, which can be found in any hardware store. Figure 5-1 shows a LEGO version of a ratchet mechanism, which allows a spin handle to rotate in one direction, but not in the opposite direction. A gear is adapted here for

© Grady Koch 2023
G. Koch, *Learn Engineering with LEGO*, Maker Innovations Series,
https://doi.org/10.1007/978-1-4842-9280-8_5

the Ratchet, using the teeth of the gear to prevent rotation in one direction by catching against a connector. A rubber band, part of the Robot Inventor set, keeps the connector pressed up against the teeth of the gear. Building instructions follow Figure 5-1.

Figure 5-1. *The Ratchet allows for a spin handle to rotate in one direction, but not the other direction*

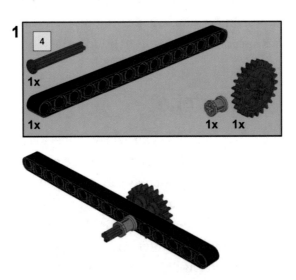

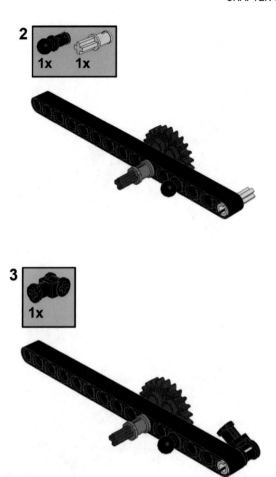

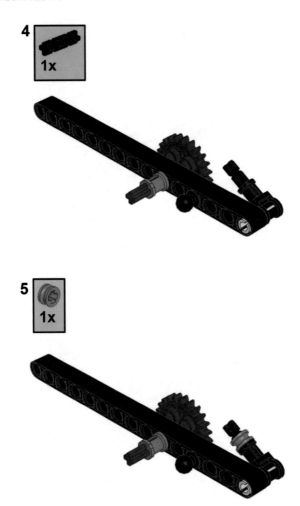

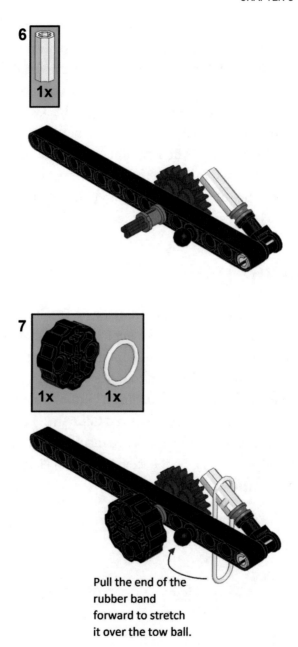

Pull the end of the
rubber band
forward to stretch
it over the tow ball.

Spinning the handle of the Ratchet should show that it can rotate in only one direction. In the allowed direction, the Ratchet makes a satisfying clicking sound, like a cricket, if the spin handle is turned quickly. A ratchet mechanism can be useful in many LEGO inventions, such as for preventing a wheeled robot or vehicle from rolling backward. Or for a LEGO model crane that lifts heavy objects, a ratchet can ensure the load doesn't fall as it's being lifted. When building a LEGO catapult, a stretched rubber band could be used to propel the catapult's arm. In such a design, a ratchet could allow the rubber band to be stretched until ready to shoot by unlocking the catch that grabs the gear's teeth.

Exercise: The Cam

A *cam* is a mechanism that provides a nudging or light lifting motion from a rotating power source, like a motor or engine. In cars that have gasoline or diesel engines, cams are hard at work opening valves to allow fuel into the engine and let exhaust out of it. In robotics, a cam is useful for an action that mimics a human finger pushing a button, which will be used later in this chapter to build the Mechanized Cannon.

But cams can be hard to see at work in a machine, since they're often buried deep in the machinery. So the exercise shown Figure 5-2 is of a cam to explore how they work.

Figure 5-2. *The axle end of the Cam creates a pushing motion as the spin handle is rotated*

The Cam uses a gear, but not for a typical gear function; instead, it acts as a circle with an off-center axle attachment point. When rotated on an axle, one end of the circle is at a farther distance from the axle than the other end of the circle. So, as the circle spins on the axle, one end of the circle reaches out farther than the other end of the circle. In the Robot Inventor set, there are two building elements that can serve as a cam: the 36-tooth gear (used in this exercise) or the round connector block.

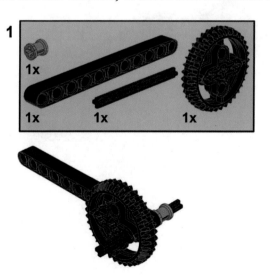

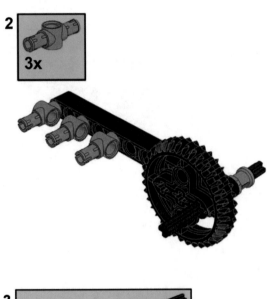

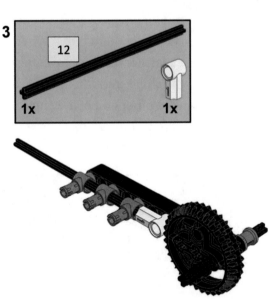

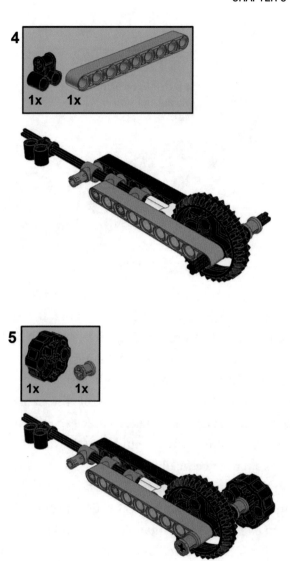

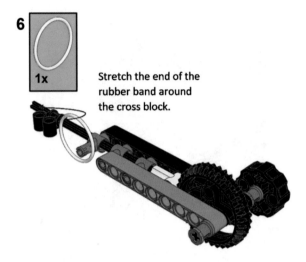

6 1x

Stretch the end of the
rubber band around
the cross block.

Turning the Cam's spin handle makes the axle move in and out. The
rubber band continuously pulls the axle back so that the axle is always
pressed up against the off-center rotating circle. The cam is similar to the
eccentric built in Chapter 3, the difference being that the cam needs a
spring (in the form of a rubber band) to work. Also, an eccentric can be
made to push with more force than a cam. While the Cam used a gear
for an off-center circle, LEGO also makes a piece specifically for a cam
described in Figure 5-3, but it's not included in the Robot Inventor set.

LEGO makes a part specifically for a cam, shown in Figure 5-3, but it's
not included in the Robot Inventor set. It can be found as part number
6575 on aftermarket parts dealers such as bricklink.com. The advantage
of the #6575 cam over using a circular element is that the #6575 cam
has three possible off-center axle attachment points to give flexibility in
choosing the length of the pushing action that the cam can apply, whereas
a circular element only has one axle attachment point.

Figure 5-3. *It's not part of the Robot Inventor, but the #6575 cam can be a good alternative to using a circular element*

Exercise: The Differential

A *differential* is a mechanism for use with wheeled vehicles that solves a common problem with controlling a vehicle in a turn. If a vehicle uses a pair of wheels, or more than one pair, a problem arises when the vehicle is in a turn, as diagrammed in Figure 5-4. In a turn, one wheel is called on to turn slower than the other wheel due to the curve involved, because one wheel travels a shorter distance. But the wheels, being driven by the same motor source in the example of Figure 5-4, can only move at the same speed. The vehicle then has a problem in the turn, likely with a skid sideways and jerky motion. The differential solves this problem, by allowing one wheel to slow down when needed, such as in a curve. When the curving turn is over, the differential automatically switches back to both wheels being run at the same speed.

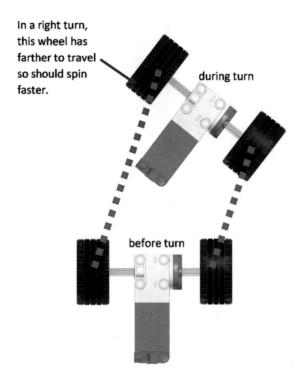

In a right turn, this wheel has farther to travel so should spin faster.

during turn

before turn

Figure 5-4. *During a turn, one wheel of a pair has to travel a farther distance than the other wheel*

The differential works by halving an axle into two pieces, with each axle having a wheel on one end and a gear on the end inside the differential. Gears inside the differential split up the torque coming into the differential in such a way that one axle can be given less speed than the other axle.

Assembling the Differential

A differential is a bit complicated to build from scratch with gears and building elements, so LEGO provides a premade differential in the Robot Inventor set, as shown in Figure 5-5. The LEGO differential comes in pieces, though, requiring assembly as per the instructions that follow the figure.

Figure 5-5. *The assembled differential*

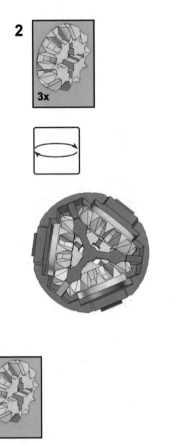

2

3x

3

1x

This gear should lay flat against the three gears beneath it, with the gears' teeth meshed all the way around.

The Differential Demonstrator

Now that the differential has been assembled, its use can be explored by building the Differential Demonstrator pictured in Figure 5-6. A motor spins a pair of wheels in the Differential Demonstrator, allowing experimentation with the idea of how one wheel can be slowed down.

Figure 5-6. *The Differential Demonstrator uses a motor to spin the differential*

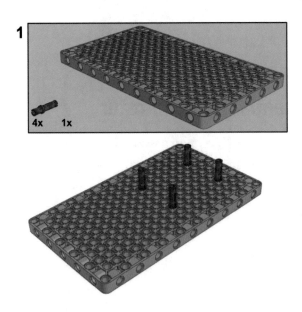

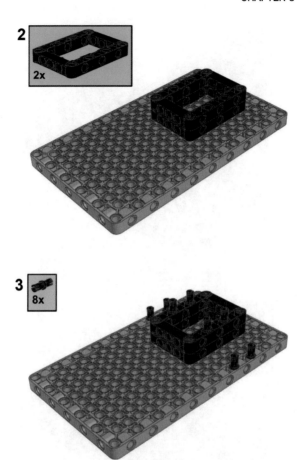

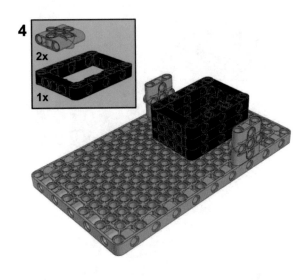

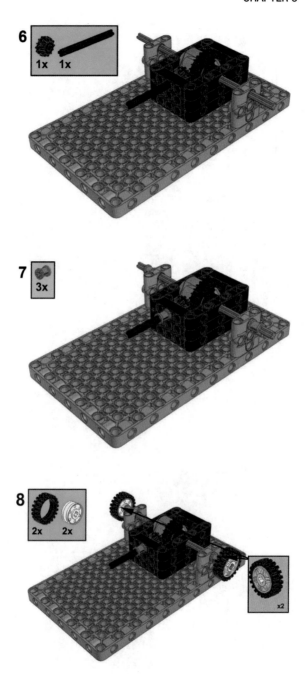

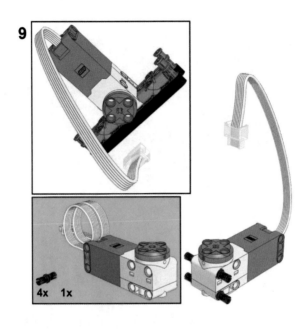

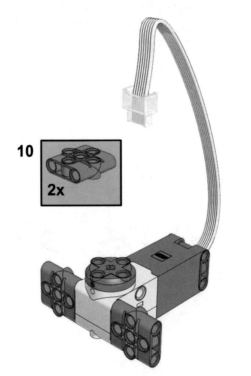

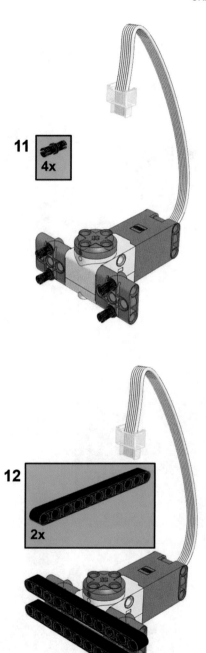

13

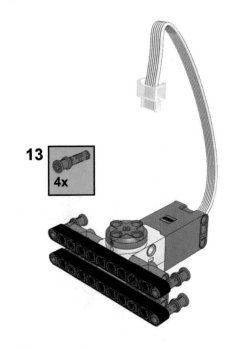

14

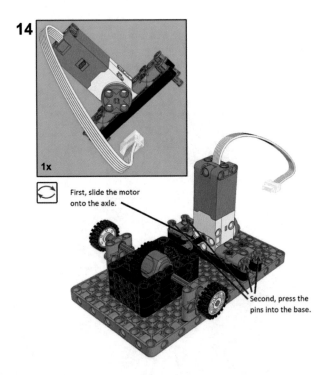

First, slide the motor
onto the axle.

Second, press the
pins into the base.

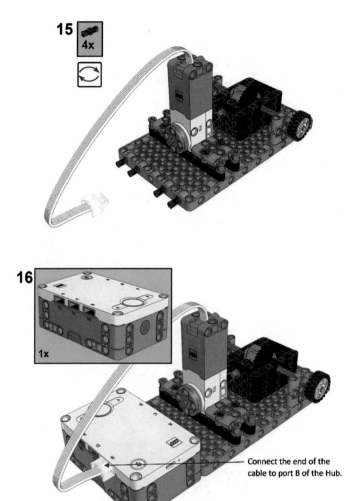

Connect the end of the
cable to port B of the Hub.

The Differential Demonstrator can be activated to set the two wheels
in motion by turning on the motor using the Hub. Details on running a
motor with the Hub can be found in Chapter 1. With the wheels spinning,
pressing with a finger on one wheel results in the wheel slowing down. And
the harder this wheel is pressed, the more it will slow. But while pressing
on this one wheel, the other wheel keeps on spinning at the same speed.

Releasing the pressed wheel will have it go back to its prior speed. This shows that the differential acts as a speed reducer for one wheel of the pair when one wheel is called on to slow down. When used on a wheeled vehicle or robot, such a one-wheel speed reduction is needed anytime a turn is made. So driving is made much smoother using a differential.

Exercise: Turntables

A *turntable* is a mechanism that provides a platform for rotation. Old-fashioned record players use a turntable to spin vinyl records. Another example of a turntable, sometimes called a *Lazy Susan*, is in a kitchen cabinet for more convenient use of space. And giant turntables are used in train terminals to reverse the direction of locomotives. In the realm of LEGO, a turntable can be useful for aiming a sensor or turning the head of a robot. The Robot Inventor set includes two types of turntables, shown in Figure 5-7, with one large turntable and two small turntables. Each turntable comes in two pieces in the set, as shown in Figure 5-8, that are pressed together to look like Figure 5-7.

Figure 5-7. *The Robot Inventor set includes three turntables: one large and two small*

Figure 5-8. *Each of the turntables comes in two parts that are pressed together to assemble*

The turntables have teeth around their rims that can mesh with a gear, so gears are a good way to get a turntable moving. A gear can be meshed with a turntable either along a straight line or at a right angle. Both of these meshing techniques are used in the Turntable Playground of Figure 5-9. Three turntables are put into action in the Turntable Playground, used to give minifigures a fun ride. One turntable spins continuously, and an interesting twist is used for the other two turntables to have them spin in intermittent motion using a gear mounted off center. *Intermittent* means that the motion is on and off, in contrast to continuous movement.

Figure 5-9. *The Turntable Playground gives a ride to minifigures*

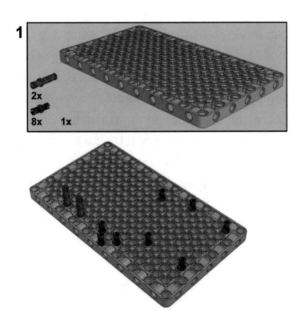

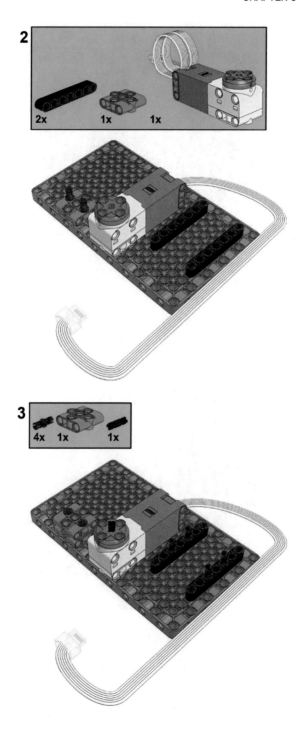

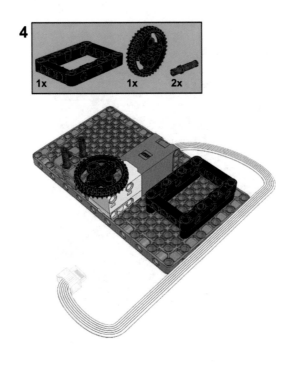

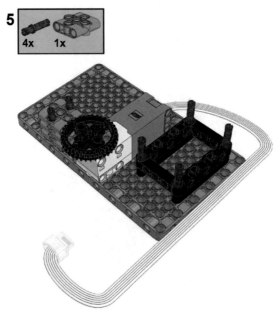

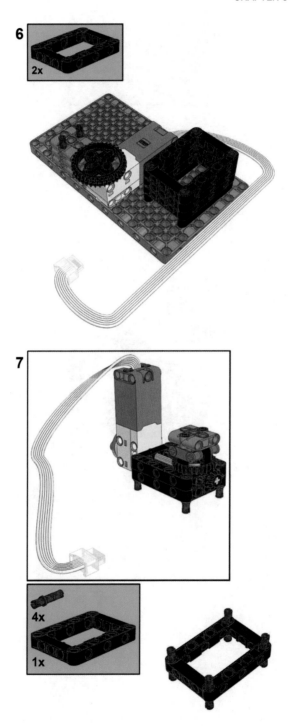

185

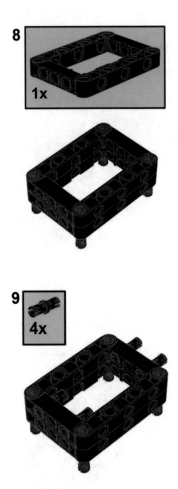

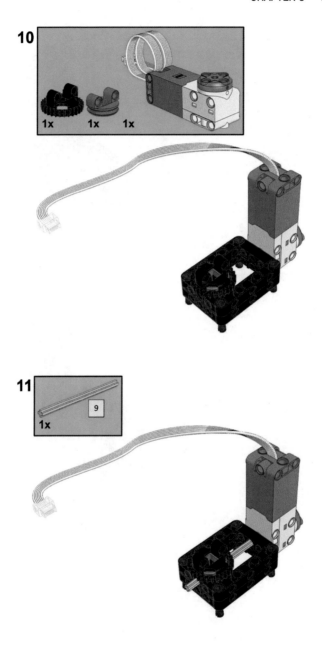

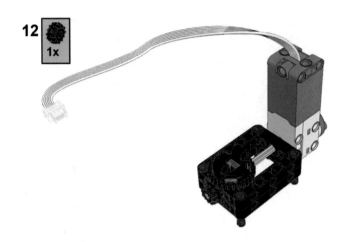

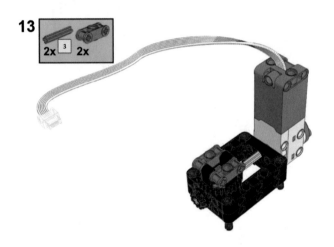

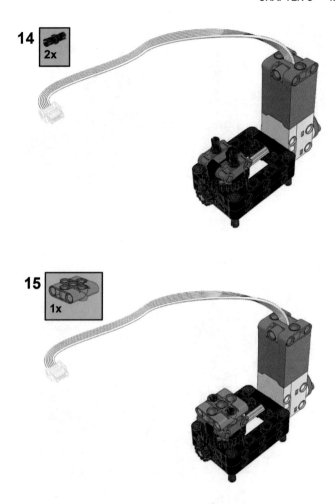

14 2x

15 1x

16

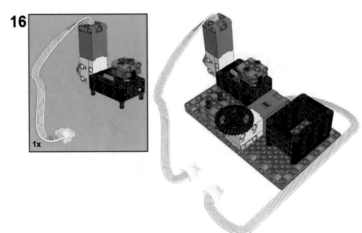

17

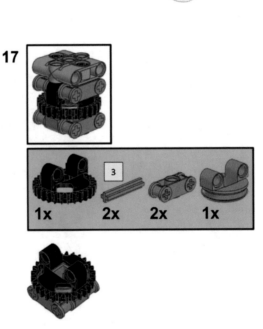

21

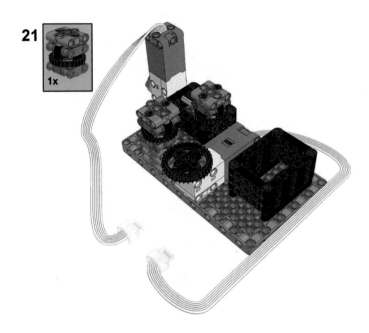

22

Also insert two pins on
the other side of the
liftarm stack at
matching locations.

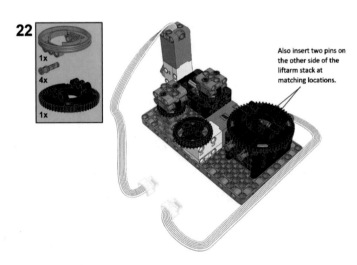

23

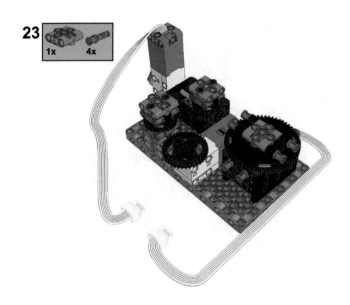

24

These pins provide
attachments for minifigures.

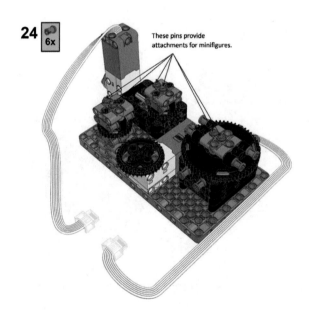

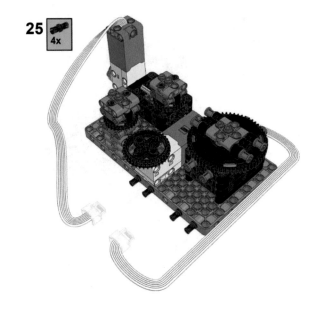

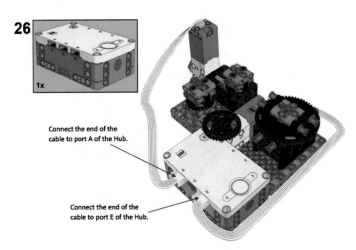

Connect the end of the cable to port A of the Hub.

Connect the end of the cable to port E of the Hub.

The turntables can be set in motion by control from the Hub, as described in Chapter 1. This exercise is a little different in motor control in that two motors are involved, with the Hub's controls applied to both motors.

Project: The Mechanized Cannon

The final project of this chapter shows that mechanisms can be combined together in a machine, in this case to build the Mechanized Cannon of Figure 5-10. The Mechanized Cannon can aim with a spin handle, then shoot off a dart by activating a motor. The mechanisms involved include a turntable to aim the cannon and a cam to press a button to trigger a dart shooter. The dart shooter is also a mechanism, though a fully contained one and not something to be built from scratch. The Robot Inventor set includes two dart shooters, along with the darts. The dart shooter has a button on the back to trigger shooting, which can be tried out by loading a dart into the front of the shooter and then pressing the button, but making sure that the dart is pointed away from the operator or anyone else. Instead of manual shooting, the Mechanized Cannon automates control of the dart shooter by triggering the shooter with a motor-driven cam mechanism. The cam mechanism is similar to the design built earlier in this chapter, except for the use of a round connector block in place of the gear in order to make the cam smaller. Like the gear, the round connector block has an off-center axle mounting hole, so it can be used to build a cam. The cam in this design doesn't use a rubber band like the cam built in the exercise earlier in this chapter. The rubber band isn't needed here, because there's a spring inside the dart shooter that serves the same function as the rubber band: keeping the cam's pusher up against the rotating gear. There's a large rectangular liftarm at the back of the Mechanized Cannon that acts as a safety feature to prevent two accidents: aiming a dart at the operator and spinning the turntable so far that the motor's cable gets pulled too far.

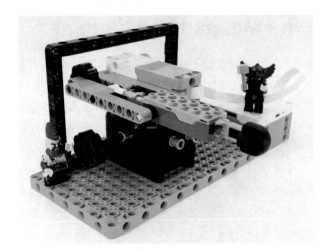

Figure 5-10. *The Mechanized Cannon aims with a spin handle to shoot a dart*

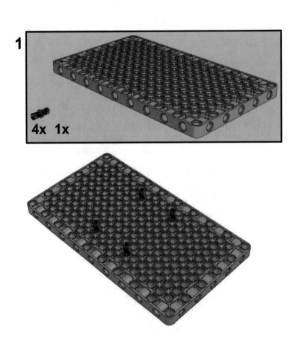

2 **2x**

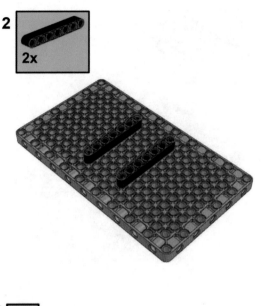

3 **4x**

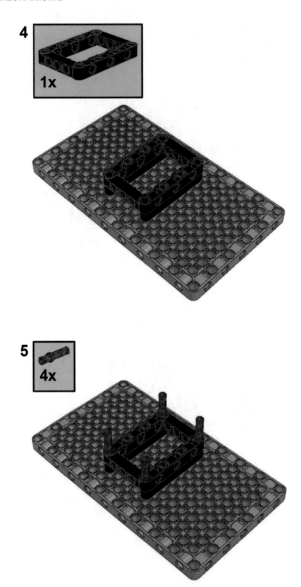

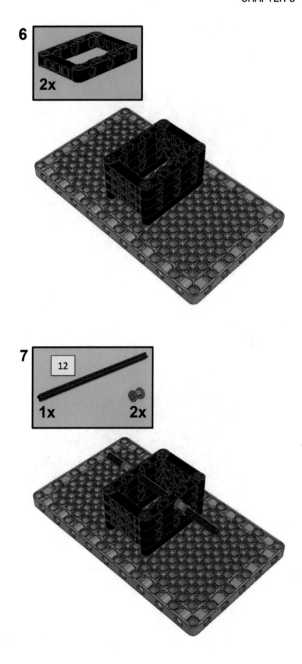

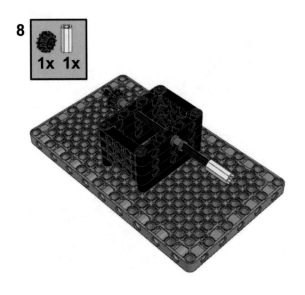

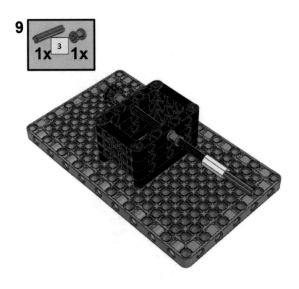

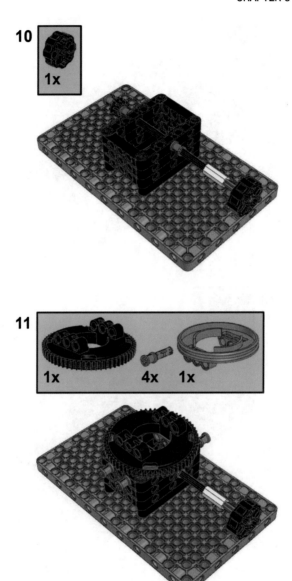

12 4x

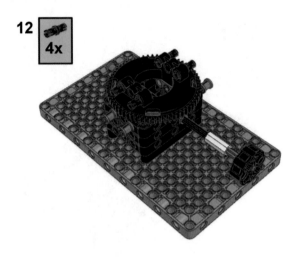

13 2x

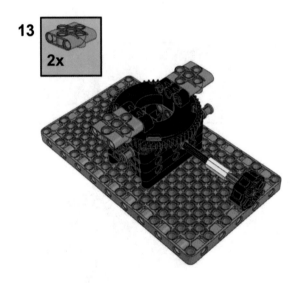

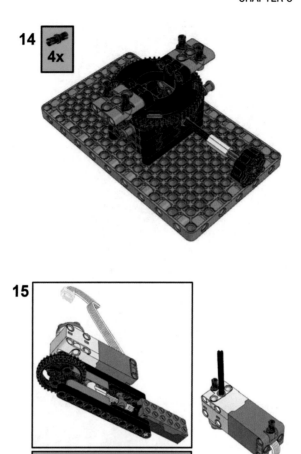

17

18

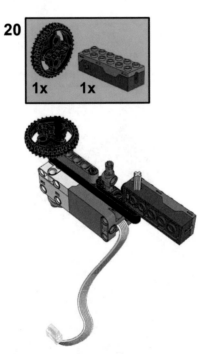

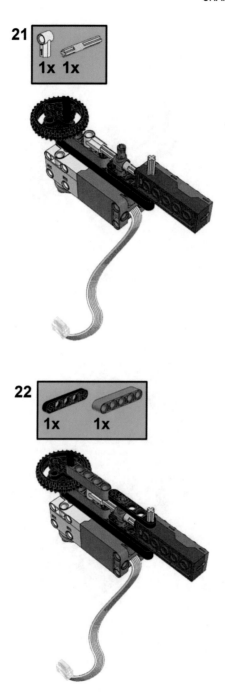

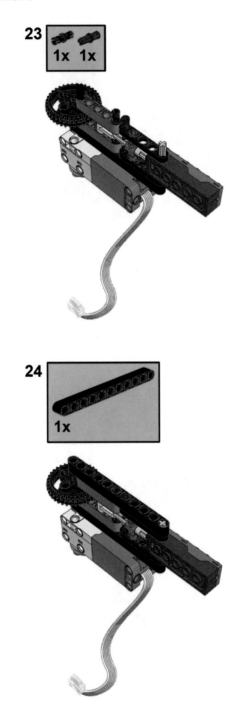

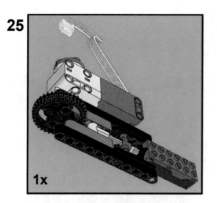

25

1x

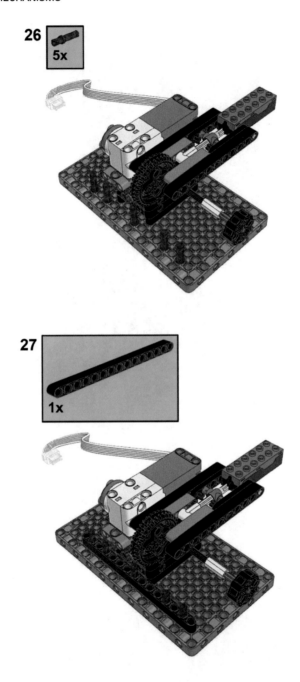

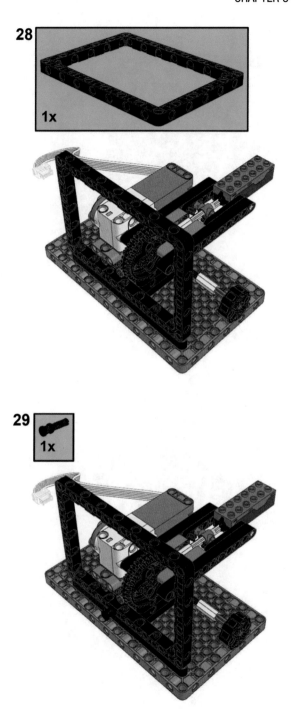

30

31

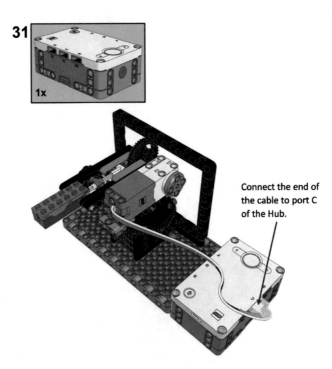

Connect the end of
the cable to port C
of the Hub.

The Mechanized Cannon is used by placing it on a table with the dart pointing away from anyone. Powering up the Hub and pressing the center button will prepare the motor. The dart can then be aimed by turning the spin handle that drives the turntable. Once lined up with a target, a dart can be fired by pressing either the left or right button on the Hub. Now that a means has been built to activate the dart shooter with motorized control, an extension may be to have a computer or robot decide when to shoot a dart. This idea will be implemented in Chapter 8.

Summary

This chapter explored the design and use of mechanisms, systems of parts working together in a machine to create a specific action like lifting, spinning, pushing, nudging, driving, or shooting. Four example mechanisms were built of a ratchet, cam, differential, and turntable, which can be useful for building custom inventions. These mechanisms showed that

- A ratchet allows rotation in only one direction.

- A cam gives a light pushing motion from a rotational power source.

- A differential allows one wheel of a pair to slow down when needed, such as in a turn.

- A turntable provides a platform for rotation.

Some mechanisms, such as the example exercise of the Ratchet and Cam, can be built from scratch from parts in the Robot Inventor set. Other mechanisms, such as the differential and turntable, use parts made by LEGO specifically for use in a mechanism. The final project of this chapter combined several mechanisms to build a Mechanized Cannon. Mechanisms are often used in inventions, as will be seen in the projects of upcoming chapters.

CHAPTER 6

Motors

Motors are devices that use electrical power to create mechanical rotation. With a LEGO motor, an axle can be inserted in the motor to make use of the revolution to, for example, spin the wheels of a robot or vehicle. But the motors have extra functionality: as *servo* motors, they are capable of precisely moving to a specific angle using a sensor inside the motor that monitors its angle and speed. The Hub uses the sensor embedded into the motor to allow setting the angular position of the motor's rotation or set the motor's speed. The exercises and project in this chapter show how to take advantage of the Robot Inventor motor's capability for powering wheels, precise angular movement, and rotation sensing.

Speed and Angle

The Robot Inventor's motors allow control of two important parameters of the motor's motion: speed and angle. Speed is how fast the motor rotates, whether clockwise or counterclockwise, with a value ranging from 0 to 100. Angle is the position of the motor's rotating part or of an axle inserted into the motor. Angle is measured in degrees, such that if it spun in a full circle, it would travel from 0 to 360 degrees. A circle on the motor's housing marks the zero-degree point, as shown in Figure 6-1. The zero-degree point can be important in some inventions because the parts attached to the motor may need to be in a specific orientation relative to the motor's position. It's possible to misalign the motor's zero point. For example, the motor could be activated without any software using the technique from Chapter 1.

© Grady Koch 2023
G. Koch, *Learn Engineering with LEGO*, Maker Innovations Series,
https://doi.org/10.1007/978-1-4842-9280-8_6

When done using the motor, it's quite likely that the motor didn't stop at its zero position. Thus, the need may arise to reset the motor's angle to zero before attaching other LEGO parts to the motor. This can be done by taking hold of the motor's rotating part and manually turning it with until the dot lines up with the circle. Another way to set the motor at its zero point is by using code commands you'll see later in this chapter, but this technique requires connection of the motor to the Hub and writing of code.

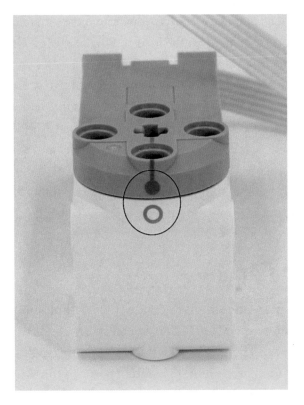

Figure 6-1. *The motor's zero position indicator*

Exercise: The Speed and Angle Demonstrator

The Speed and Angle Demonstrator, shown in Figure 6-2, serves as an introduction to working with motors. In following sections, this demonstrator will be used to explore programs that control the speed and angle of a motor. Building instructions for the Speed and Angle Demonstrator follow Figure 6-2.

Figure 6-2. *The Speed and Angle Demonstrator*

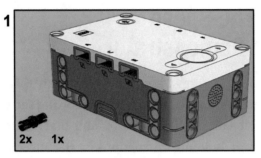

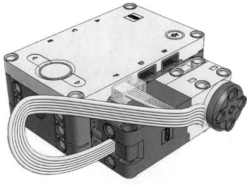

3 **2x**

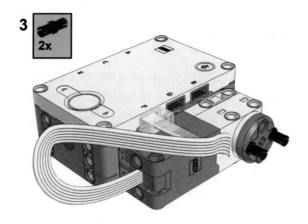

4 **1x**

Connect the end
of the cable to
port F of the Hub.

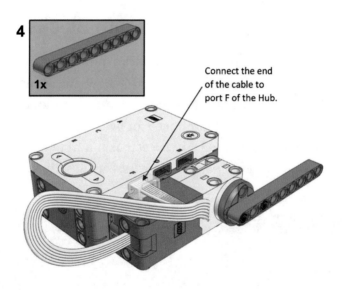

REVOLUTIONS PER MINUTE

Although the Robot Inventor measures motor speed as a value out of 100, or a percent of the maximum speed, another common way to describe motor speed is by *revolutions per minute (RPM)*. RPM is an indicator of how many times the motor completes a full rotation over a time span of one minute. For example, the Medium Motor that comes in the Robot Inventor set has a maximum RPM of 135, so a 100 percent speed setting in a program corresponds to an RPM of 135.

Controlling Motor Speed in Word Blocks

The Speed and Angle Demonstrator provides a framework for experimenting with motor control. Figure 6-3 shows how to do so in Word Blocks. This program will make the Speed and Angle Demonstrator's motor spin clockwise at maximum speed for five seconds, pause for one second, then spin counterclockwise at maximum speed for another five seconds. Word Blocks of particular interest are described following Figure 6-3.

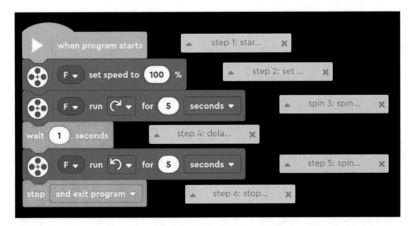

Figure 6-3. *Setting motor speed in Word Blocks*

- Step 2: The set speed to block assigns a speed setting to the motor. Any following blocks that operate a motor will use this setting. Without this block, a motor will use a default speed of 75 percent.

- Step 3: The run for block turns on the motor with user selection for the port to which the motor is connected, direction of rotation, and duration. The motor will run at the speed set in step 2.

- Step 4: The wait block pauses the spinning of the motor. This pause keeps the motor from jerky motion before the next motor command of step 5.

Controlling Motor Speed in Python

The following Python code is identical in function to the previous Word Blocks code. To indicate the direction of rotation in Python, the speed value is indicated with either a positive or negative sign to signify clockwise or counterclockwise, respectively.

```
from mindstorms import MSHub, Motor, ...
from mindstorms.control import wait_for_seconds, ...
from mindstorms.operator import greater_than, ...
import math
import hub
from sys import exit

#Create your objects here.
myhub = MSHub()
1 motor = Motor('F')
```

```
# Program "speed_demo". Spin motor clockwise, then
counterclockwise
2 motor.run_for_seconds(5,100)
wait_for_seconds(1)
3 motor.run_for_seconds(5,-100)
exit()
```

The code begins by importing modules and creating a myhub object, as in all the Python code in this book. Next, an object is created to represent the motor 1. Motor() is a module within the mindstorms package imported in the first line of code, and to enable use it's given a variable name: motor. The Hub's port, on which the motor is connected, is specified inside the parentheses of Motor()—in this case, port F. Now the functions associated with the motor can be conveniently used, as seen in the next few lines of the program.

A motor can be turned on at a constant speed with the motor object's run_for_seconds() function 2. This function runs the motor for the duration in seconds that are specified as the first number in parentheses, five seconds in this case. The second number in parentheses is the speed setting, set to 100 here for maximum speed. The speed setting can also be negative, which means that the rotation will be counterclockwise. After a one-second pause, a counterclockwise spin comes next 3.

Setting Motor Angle in Word Blocks

While the previous section described setting speed, the other basic parameter to work with is setting the motor's angle position. An option for setting the angle is the direction for going to the specified angle: clockwise, counterclockwise, or in the shortest direction. For the shortest direction selection, the motor chooses whichever direction is the quickest to reach its destination.

To demonstrate working with angle setting, Figure 6-4 shows Word Blocks code to make the motor rotate clockwise to angle 90 degrees, pause for one second, rotate counterclockwise to 0 degrees, pause again for one second, rotate counterclockwise to 270 degrees, pause once more, then rotate clockwise to home zero position. The speed setting is put at 50 to avoid jerky motion. Word Blocks of new interest are described following Figure 6-4.

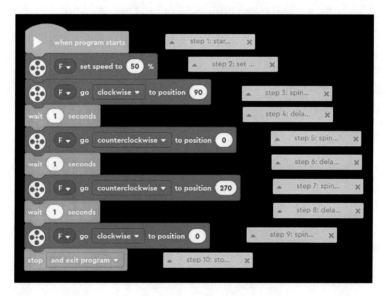

Figure 6-4. *Setting motor angle in Word Blocks*

- Step 3: The go to position block sets the motor's angle to the position specified. Other input parameters include the port that the motor is connected to and the direction in which the motor should rotate as it travels to the specified position. The motor will move at the speed set in step 2. This block is used again in steps 5, 7, and 9 to position the motor at various angle settings.

- Step 4: The wait block pauses action in the program to let the angle dwell at a position specified in the previous block. Such a wait block is also used in steps 6 and 8 to also pause at new motor settings.

Setting Motor Angle in Python

The Python code to select a motor angle begins in the same way as the speed demonstration program, including the creation of a motor object 1:

```
from mindstorms import MSHub, Motor, . . .
from mindstorms.control import wait_for_seconds, . . .
from mindstorms.operator import greater_than, . . .
import math
import hub
from sys import exit

#Create your objects here.
myhub = MSHub()
1 motor = Motor('F')

# Program "speed_demo". Spin motor clockwise, then
counterclockwise
2 motor.run_to_position(90,'clockwise',50)
wait_for_seconds(1)
motor.run_to_position(0,'counterclockwise',50)
wait_for_seconds(1)
motor.run_to_position(270,'counterclockwise',50)
wait_for_seconds(1)
motor.run_to_position(0,'clockwise',50)
wait_for_seconds(1)
exit()
```

The motor's `run_to_position()` function 2 is used repeatedly in the program to set various angle settings. This function takes three parameters in parentheses. The first is the angle to which the motor should rotate. The second parameter is the direction of the rotation: 'clockwise', 'counterclockwise', or 'shortest path'. The third parameter is the speed of the rotation to the specified angle. A dwell time at each angle setting is made by pausing action with the `wait_for_seconds()`.

Exercise: Understanding Torque and Stall

Motors have a limit to the amount of force, called torque, that they can spin with. If a task is to move something heavy with a motor, then a powerful motor is needed to apply high torque. Chapter 4 introduced the idea of torque, showing that gears need a certain amount of torque to get a gear system moving. In the experiments of Chapter 4, torque was supplied turning a crank. Instead of the crank, a motor can be attached to a gear system or machine to apply torque using electrical power. But there's a limit on how much torque a motor can supply.

The effect of a motor's torque limit can be explored by installing a liftarm on the Speed and Angle Demonstrator, as shown in Figure 6-5. Building instructions follow the figure, starting at step 5 from where the Speed and Angle Demonstrator left off. The installed liftarm will block the rotation of the motor, which is ordinarily a situation to be avoided. But in this case, the idea is to purposely block the motor to experiment with torque.

Figure 6-5. *A liftarm is added to the Speed and Angle Demonstrator to block rotation of the motor*

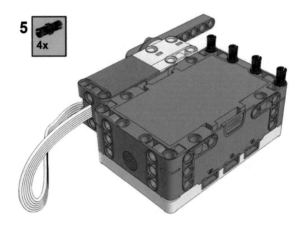

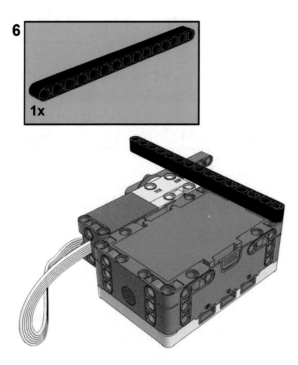

With the liftarm now installed to the Speed and Angle Demonstrator, running the program for setting motor speed will show that the motor jams up against the blocking liftarm. This situation of the motor becoming stuck is called *stall*. After a pause, the motor will spin around in the opposite direction to again stall against the liftarm. Whichever direction the motor goes, it can't push off the blocking liftarm because there isn't enough torque to do so.

This exercise also shows that each time the motor stalls against the blocking liftarm, the motor will push for about two seconds, then back off and stop trying to push. This automatic shutoff is a safety feature built into the motor to prevent the motor, or whatever object is being pushed on, from being damaged. This safety feature can be shut off with advanced programming, but it's best to keep the automatic stall shutoff until more is learned about using motors.

THE LARGE MOTOR

The Robot Inventor set comes with Medium Motors, but LEGO also makes a higher torque motor called the Large Motor that works with the Hub—the same programming Word Blocks or Python functions can be used for either motor. The Large Motor has 2.3 times higher torque than the Medium Motor.

Exercise: Powering a Vehicle with a Tank Drive

One way to build a vehicle or mobile robot is to use two motors side by side, with a wheel attached to each motor. This type of vehicle propulsion is called tank drive. The name comes from the use of the drive in military tanks, with a motor on each side driving a tread so the tank can go over rugged terrain. Construction vehicles, like bulldozers and excavators, also use tank drive. Tank drive is commonly used in robots, not just LEGO robots, but all sorts of mobile robots. To go forward or backward with a tank drive, both motors spin. To go left or right, one motor spins while the other motor is still. Or to spin in a fast turn, one motor goes clockwise and the other motor goes counterclockwise. The Tank, shown in Figure 6-6, illustrates these features of tank drive.

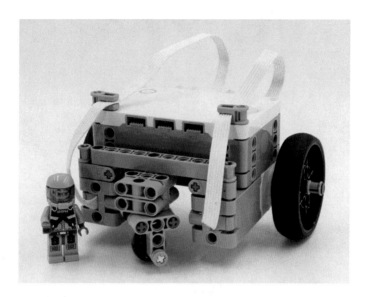

Figure 6-6. *The Tank uses a pair of motors that each drive a wheel*

Building the Tank

Three wheels are involved with the Tank, with two large wheels driven by motors and a third wheel to give balance to the Tank. Without the third wheel, the Tank would fall over. This balancing wheel is a design called a *caster*, which has the ability to pivot to align with the direction of the Tank's travel. Casters can be seen in action in everyday life on shopping carts and desk office chairs. A LEGO caster is part of the Tank building instructions, at steps 13–18.

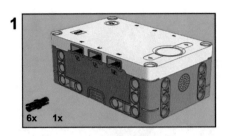

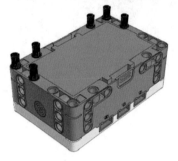

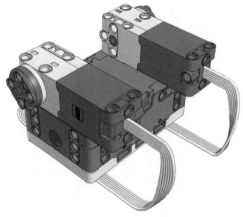

3

4x

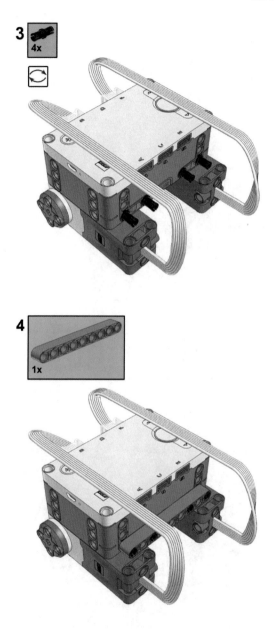

4

1x

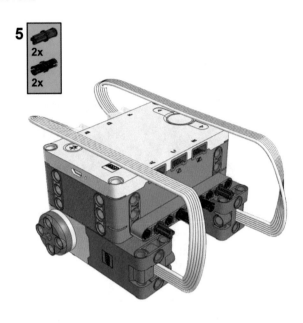

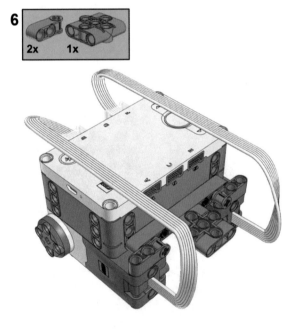

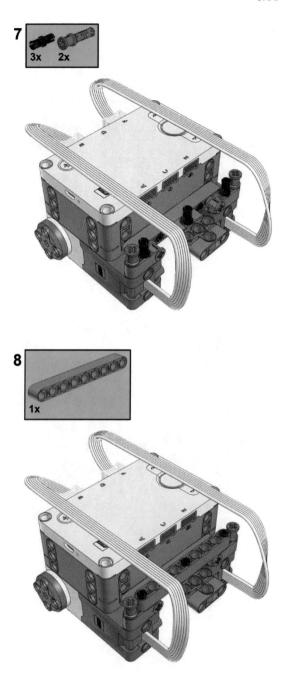

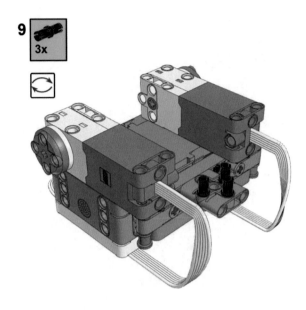

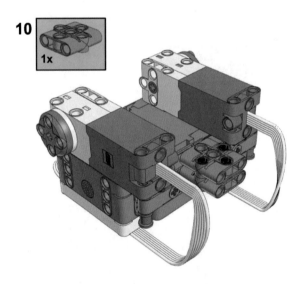

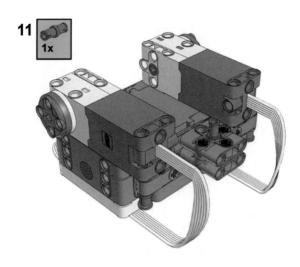

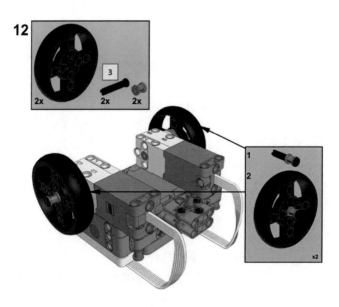

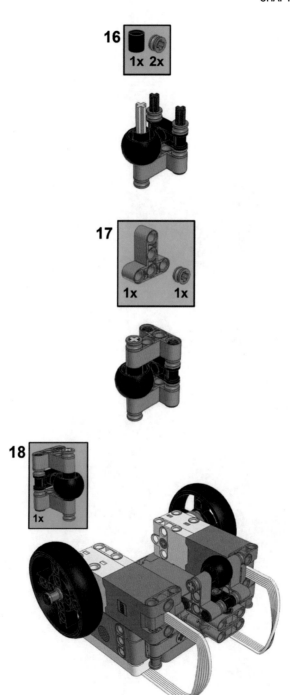

19 2x

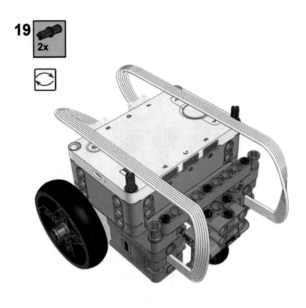

Pass the cable through the wire connector and connect the end of the cable to port B of the Hub.

Pass the cable through the wire connector and connect the end of the cable to port F of the Hub.

20 2x

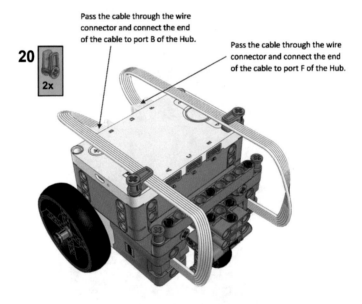

Programming the Tank

The Tank's drive wheels are each connected to a motor, and controlling each motor allows maneuverability. An advantage of the Tank is that it can move in confined spaces, which is why tank drive is commonly used in robots. This maneuverability can be seen by solving the problem statement:

> Spin the Tank clockwise for five seconds, then
> move forward for two seconds, and backward for
> two seconds. Finally, spin counterclockwise for
> five seconds. Between each maneuver, pause for
> one second.

Forward is assumed to be the direction opposite the caster. In other words, the caster is on the back side of the Tank. The algorithm to solve this problem is as follows:

1. Start the program.

2. Assign motors to port B for the left motor and port F for the right motor.

3. Spin clockwise for five seconds.

4. Delay for one second.

5. Move forward for two seconds.

6. Delay for one second.

7. Move backward for two seconds.

8. Delay for one second.

9. Spin counterclockwise for five seconds.

10. Stop the program.

The flowchart implementation for this algorithm is shown in Figure 6-7.

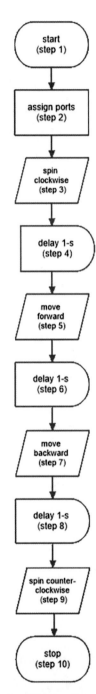

Figure 6-7. *Flowchart for the Tank algorithm*

The Word Blocks Code

The Word Blocks code for the Tank algorithm is shown in Figure 6-8, with ten blocks that match the steps of the algorithm and flowchart. Motor movement is by blocks that involve a pair of motors, as indicated by the icon of two motors in a side-by-side arrangement.

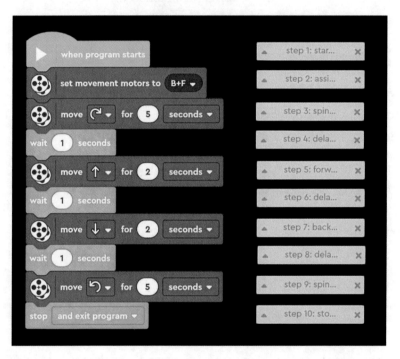

Figure 6-8. *Word Blocks code to drive the Tank*

- Step 2: The set movement motors to assigns the ports to which the motors are attached. The left motor is on port B, and the right motor is on port F.

- Step 3: The move for block turns on both motors. This
  block includes options for distance, time, and angular
  degree, with the time option used here. Another option
  is for selection of the direction of the tank as indicated
  by an arrow, allowing selection for straight movement
  or spins. A clockwise spin is selected in this step,
  whereas blocks 5, 7, and 9 use different directions.

The Python Code

The Python code for the Tank algorithm is listed as follows. The function
for movement is called move_tank(), showing from the name of the
function that tank drive is a commonly used technique.

```
from mindstorms.control import wait_for_seconds, . . .
from mindstorms.operator import greater_than, . . .
import math
import hub
from sys import exit

#Create your objects here.
myhub = MSHub()
1 motor_pair = MotorPair('B','F')

# Program "tank_drive". Spin CW, forward, backward, spin CCW.
2motor_pair.move_tank(5,'seconds',left_speed=50,right_
speed=-50)
wait_for_seconds(1)
motor_pair.move_tank(2,'seconds',left_speed=50,right_speed=50)
wait_for_seconds(1)
motor_pair.move_tank(2,'seconds',left_speed=-50,right_speed=-50)
wait_for_seconds(1)
motor_pair.move_tank(2,'seconds',left_speed=-50,right_speed=50)
exit()
```

An object is created to represent both motors with the MotorPair() function 1, which comes from a module within the mindstorms package. The port assignment is made in parentheses, with the left motor listed first. Control of the tank drive is then made with the move_tank() function by passing it the length of time, units of seconds, left motor speed, and right motor speed in parentheses 2. For example, to make the Tank spin, both motors are given the same speed but in opposite directions. While the 'seconds' unit is used here, other possible units for this function include distance, rotations, and degrees. The end of each maneuver by the Tank is marked by pausing with a wait_for_seconds() function.

Exercise: Using a Motor As a Rotation Sensor

In addition to their function as motors to create rotation, motors in Robot Inventor also serve as rotation sensors. So a motor can measure the angle position or speed of rotation. This sensor function can come in useful, such as for using a motor as a control knob, creating a turn knob to adjust something. As an example, Figure 6-9 shows the Position Mimic, which points a liftarm to whatever angle position is dialed in on a control knob.

Figure 6-9. *The Position Mimic keeps a liftarm pointed in the same direction as the indicator on a control knob*

Building the Position Mimic

The Position Mimic uses two motors, one as a control knob and one as a pointer that orients a liftarm. The knob motor, on the left side, serves to measure the angle position of the knob. The pointer motor, on the right side, points in the same angle as the knob motor. The control knob uses a gear to allow getting a good grip when turning the knob, and an indicator attached in front of the gear on the control knob shows the angle position that the motor holding the liftarm should duplicate.

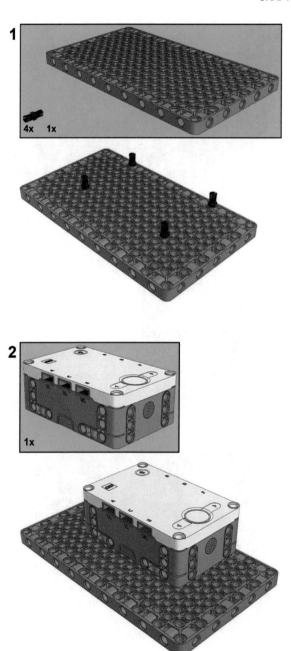

3

4

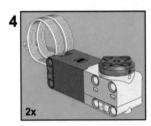

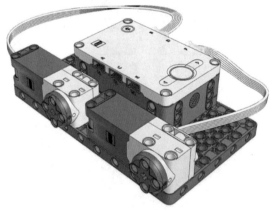

5

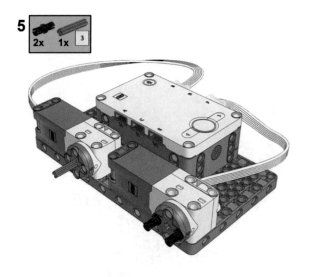

6

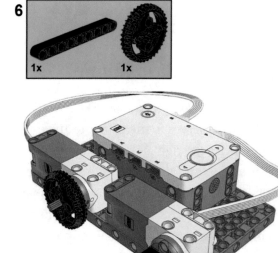

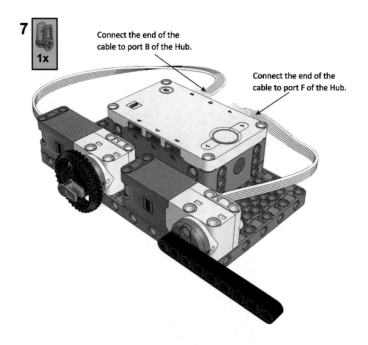

7
1x

Connect the end of the
cable to port B of the Hub.

Connect the end of the
cable to port F of the Hub.

Programming the Position Mimic

The Position Mimic involves two motors called knob and pointer. The knob motor, on the left side, serves to measure the angle position of the knob. The pointer motor, on the right side, is meant to point to the same angular position as the knob motor. Turning the knob should result in the position motor, with its attached liftarm, pointing to the same angle as the knob's indicator. Before programming the Position Mimic, it's a good idea to check that both motors are zeroed, as explained earlier in this chapter and pictured in Figure 6-1. The following problem statement explains what the Position Mimic should do:

> Make the pointer motor continuously set its angle
> to the same angle as the knob motor. Keep up the
> angular tracking until either the left or right button
> on the Hub is pressed to stop the program.

An algorithm to solve the problem statement is as follows:

1. Start the program.

2. Create a loop that repeats unless the left or right
    button is pressed. If either button is pressed, skip
    to step 4.

3. Set the angle position of the pointer motor to be the
    same as the knob motor.

4. Stop the program.

And a flowchart for this algorithm is given in Figure 6-10, which
includes a loop for indefinite operation unless a button is pressed on
the Hub.

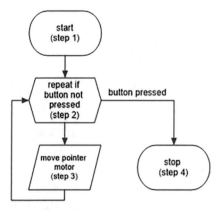

Figure 6-10. *Flowchart for the Position Mimic algorithm*

The Word Blocks Code

The Word Blocks code for the Position Mimic algorithm is shown in
Figure 6-11. Four blocks are involved, each corresponding to a step in the
algorithm.

Figure 6-11. *Word Blocks code for the Position Mimic algorithm*

Particular blocks of interest include

- Step 2: The `repeat until` block sets up a loop that repeats indefinitely until the condition is met that either the left or right button is pressed on the front. This means of stopping the program was also used in Chapter 2 for the Dance Floor.

- Step 3: The `go to position` block tells the pointer motor to go to the angle position that matches the position measured on the knob motor. In other words, this block both reads a motor (the knob motor on port B) and rotates a motor (the pointer motor on port F).

The Python Code

The Python code for the Position Mimic algorithm is listed as follows:

```python
from mindstorms import MSHub, Motor, . . .
from mindstorms.control import wait_for_seconds, . . .
from mindstorms.operator import greater_than, . . .
import math
import hub
from sys import exit
```

```
#Create your objects here.
myhub = MSHub()
1 knob = Motor('B')
2 pointer = Motor('F')

# Program "position_mimic". Make pointer angle same as
knob angle.
3 while True:
  4 if myhub.left_button.is_pressed() or myhub.right_button.
  is_pressed():
 exit()
  5 position = knob.get_position()
  6 pointer.run_to_position(position,'shortest path',75)
```

The two motors are each assigned as objects 1, 2. A while True loop is used to keep the program running indefinitely 3, unless a button is pressed on the Hub 4. This loop-until-button-pressed design was also used in Chapter 2 for the Dance Floor. Within the loop, two lines of code measure the knob motor's angle position and match this angle on the pointer motor. The knob's measured position is taken with the get_position() function and assigned the value to a variable named *position* 5. This variable then gets inserted in the run_to_position() function, which makes the pointer motor go to the same angle as the knob motor 6. The run_to_position() function takes two additional parameters: the direction, set to 'shortest path', and the motor speed. Full speed can make the pointer motor's motion jittery, so the speed is decreased to a level of 75.

Project: The Rear-Wheel Drive Car

One way to drive a vehicle was described in an earlier section, with tank drive that uses two side-by-side motors. Another way to build a steerable vehicle is to spin a pair of wheels with one motor, then use another motor as a servo to tilt another pair of wheels. This arrangement is called a *rear-wheel drive*—the rear wheels provide drive power, and the front wheels tilt to steer. Figure 6-12 shows an example with the Rear-Wheel Drive Car. Both functions of a motor described in this chapter will be used: controlling rotation and angle position.

Figure 6-12. *The Rear-Wheel Drive Car*

Building the Rear-Wheel Drive Car

Instructions to build the Rear-Wheel Drive Car are given as follows. The drive wheels, at the rear of the car, use the differential described in Chapter 5 to make smooth turns. The motors should be zeroed before their installation, as in Figure 6-1. This is especially important for the steering motor, because the direction the car will steer is referenced to the motor's zero position. In other words, the motor's zero position has the car steered to go straight.

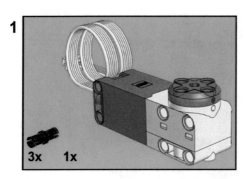

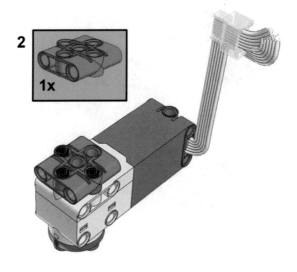

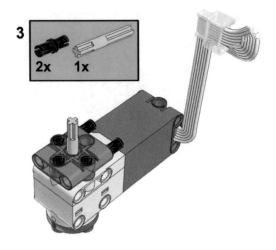

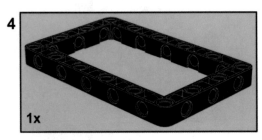

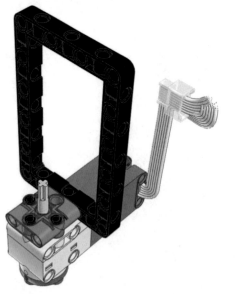

5

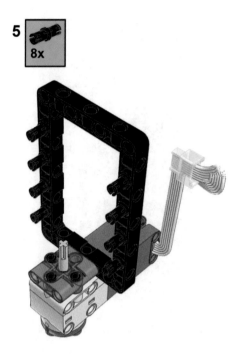

6

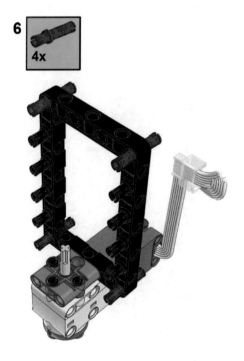

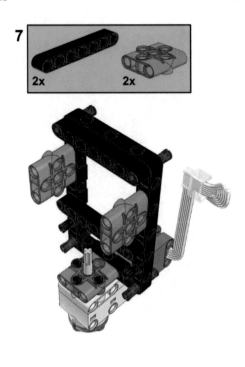

9

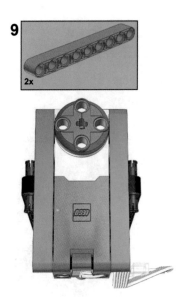

10

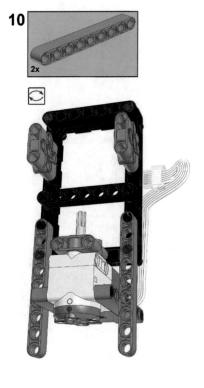

11

12

13

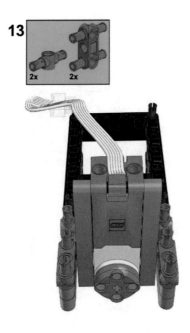

14

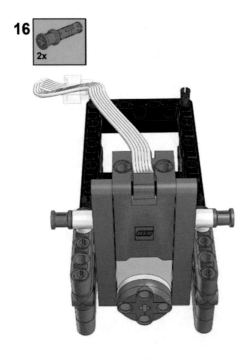

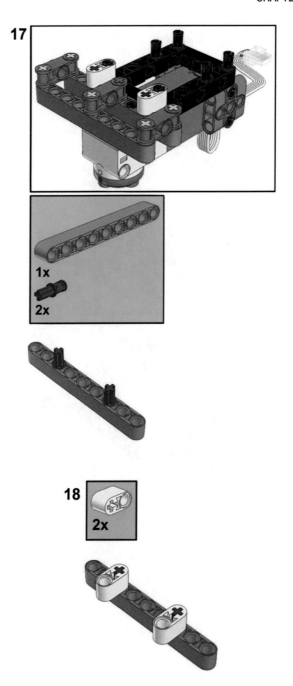

19

2x

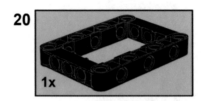

20

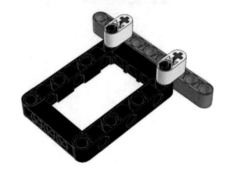

1x

21

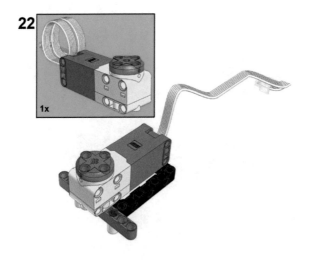

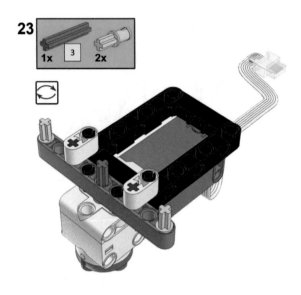

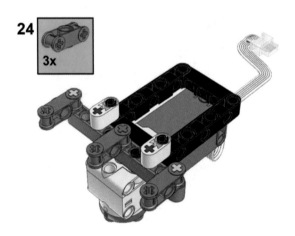

25

3x

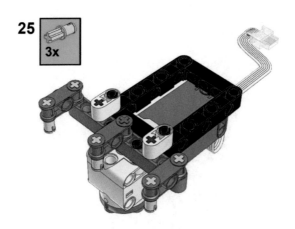

26

1x

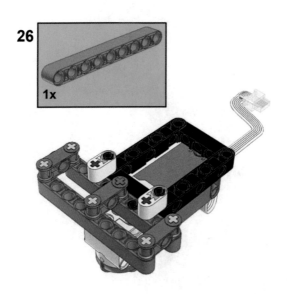

27

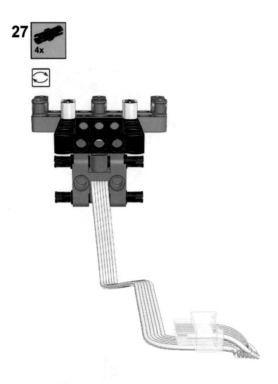

28

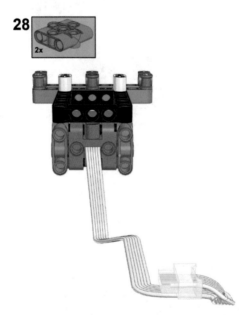

29

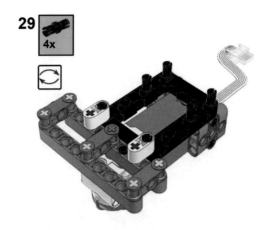

30

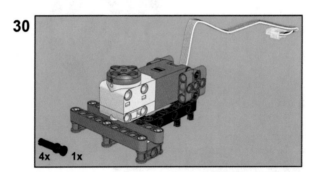

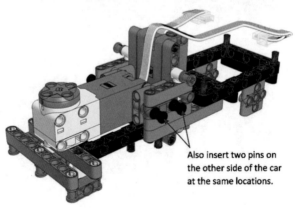

Also insert two pins on
the other side of the car
at the same locations.

31

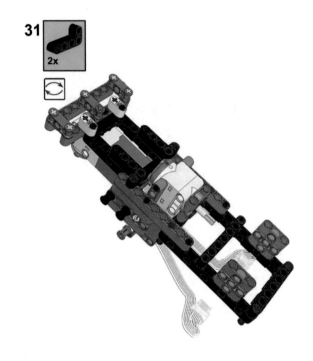

32

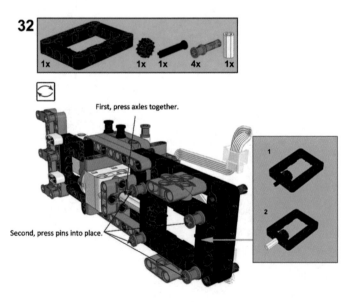

First, press axles together.

Second, press pins into place.

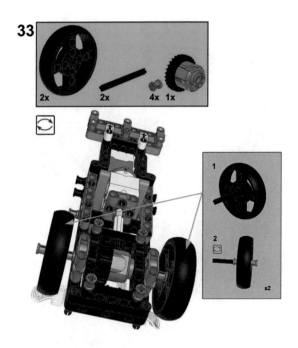

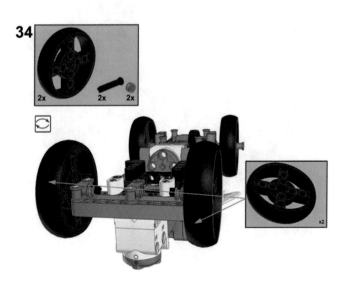

35

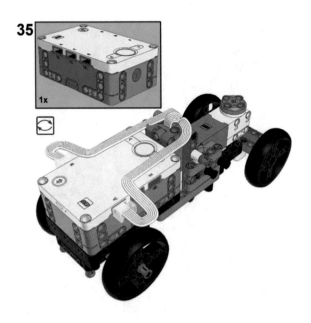

36

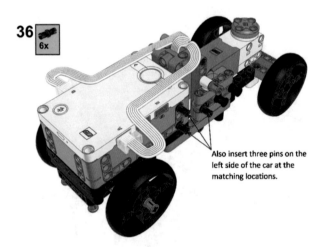

Also insert three pins on the left side of the car at the matching locations.

37

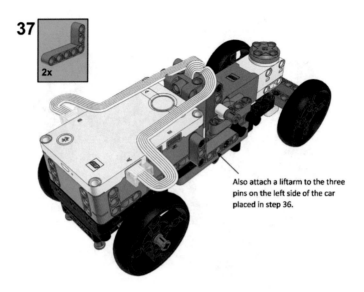

Also attach a liftarm to the three pins on the left side of the car placed in step 36.

38

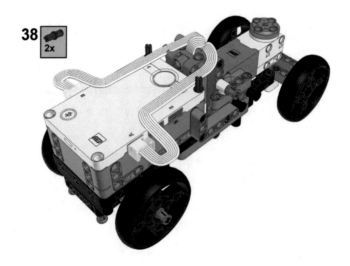

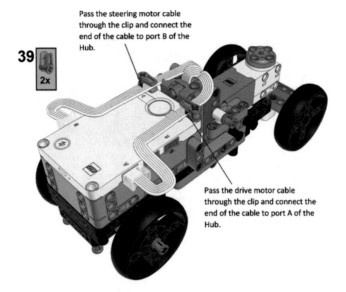

Pass the steering motor cable through the clip and connect the end of the cable to port B of the Hub.

39 2x

Pass the drive motor cable through the clip and connect the end of the cable to port A of the Hub.

Programming the Rear-Wheel Drive Car

Programming the Rear-Wheel Drive Car involves the control of two motors, with one motor to power the wheels and another motor to steer the front wheels. The following problem statement will exercise both these motors:

> Drive the car forward along a straight line for two seconds, then backward for two seconds. Repeat this motion but on a curve to the right, then repeat again for a curve to the left.

An algorithm to solve this problem is as follows:

1. Start the program.

2. Align the steering motor for straight ahead.

3. Drive forward for two seconds.

4. Drive backward for two seconds.

5. Align the steering motor for right curve.

6. Drive forward for two seconds.

7. Drive backward for two seconds.

8. Align the steering motor for left curve.

9. Drive forward for two seconds.

10. Drive backward for two seconds.

11. Stop the program.

And a flowchart implementation is shown in Figure 6-13.

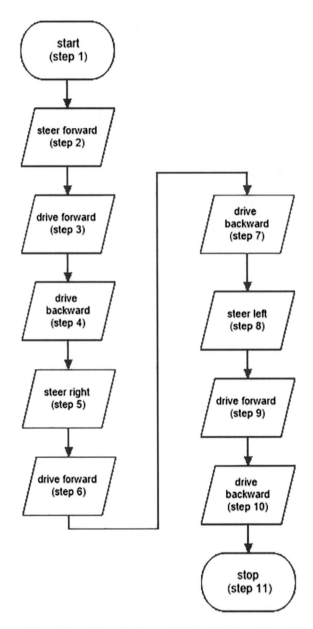

Figure 6-13. *Flowchart for the Rear-Wheel Drive Car algorithm*

The Word Blocks Code

The algorithm and flowchart indicate that operating the Rear-Wheel Drive Car involves control of two motors. One motor drives the rear wheels, with parameters to consider of the speed of rotation and the direction of rotation. The car's direction forward or backward can be changed by the direction of rotation, whether clockwise or counterclockwise, of the motor speed setting. The second motor acts as a servo on the front wheels, tilting the motor to steer the car in a particular direction. Figure 6-14 shows the Rear-Wheel Drive Car program written in Word Blocks.

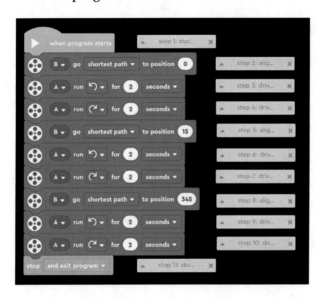

Figure 6-14. *Word Blocks code for the Rear-Wheel Drive Car*

Noteworthy blocks in the code include

- Step 2: The go to position block sets the steering motor to the zero position to align the wheels straight ahead. This block points out a couple things to double-check after building the car: the motor is zeroed and that the steering motor is connected to port B. Steps 5 and 8 also use this block, with different angle settings to steer right and left.

- Step 3: The run for block turns on the drive motor to move the car, in this case for a duration of two seconds. The counterclockwise direction setting will drive the car forward, while a clockwise setting (used in step 4) will drive the car backward. This forward and backward combination is repeated again in steps 6, 7, 9, and 10.

The Python Code

The Python code for operating the Rear-Wheel Drive Car is as follows. As with most of the code in this book, the program makes extensive use of functions:

```
from mindstorms import MSHub, Motor, . . .
from mindstorms.control import wait_for_seconds, . . .
from mindstorms.operator import greater_than, . . .
import math
import hub
from sys import exit

#Create your objects here.
myhub = MSHub()
1 drive = Motor('A')
2 steer = Motor('B')

# Program "rear_wheel". Drive straight, curve right,
curve left.
3 steer.run_to_position(0,'shortest path',50)
4 drive.run_for_seconds(2,-75)
drive.run_for_seconds(2,75)
```

```
5 steer.run_to_position(15,'shortest path',50)
drive.run_for_seconds(2,-75)
drive.run_for_seconds(2,75)
steer.run_to_position(345,'shortest path',50)
drive.run_for_seconds(2,-75)
drive.run_for_seconds(2,75)
exit()
```

There are two motors involved in the Rear-Wheel Drive Car, so objects are created for each and assigned to the variables drive and steer 1, 2. The motors' variable names indicate their functions, making the code easier to understand. The drive motor is connected to port A, and the steering motor is connected to port B.

To steer the car, the steering motor is set to a specific angle setting using the run.to.position() 3. There are three motor parameters to enter in this function: angle setting, direction of rotation, and speed of rotation. The program uses this function repeatedly; the first time it is used, the car is steered straight ahead, so set to 0 degrees. To keep the motor from spinning to a point of being blocked as the tilted wheel hits up against the car's chassis, the 'shortest path' parameter is used. Finally, using the full speed of the motor may cause the front end of the car to jerk, so a moderate 50 percent speed is a good choice.

Now that the steering direction is set, the next two lines of code drive the car forward and then backward with the run_for_seconds() function 4. This function takes two parameters: duration and motor speed. The direction of travel is specified with either a positive or negative motor speed. A forward direction for the car corresponds to a negative speed setting; hence, -75 percent for speed moves the car forward. Using a negative speed setting to move forward may seem counterintuitive. It's because the vehicle's many gears affect the direction in which the motor will direct the vehicle; the wheels in this design actually spin in the opposite direction than the motor. If a farther distance is desired, then speed can be increased to 100 percent or time duration can be increased. To move backward, a positive value for the speed should be used, in this case 75 percent.

The Rear-Wheel Drive Car can be turned by adjusting the angle of the steering motor, such as by the `run_to_position()` function to set an angle of 15 degrees 5. This angle tilts the car's front wheels toward the right. To curve to the left, this function can be used again with an angle setting of 345 degrees. The angles of steering used here are examples that can, of course, be experimented with. Also, variables could be used, such as for steering angles or durations of time to drive, to allow convenient change of these parameters in more complex programs.

Summary

This chapter explored the use of the motors that come in the Robot Inventor set. A motor can be used for both simple functions, like spinning a wheel, and complex functions, like moving to a precise angle position. Several exercises worked with motors to use these spinning and positioning functions. A motor can also be used as a rotation sensor, and another exercise used this feature to make a control knob. One of the primary uses for motors is to move a wheeled vehicle or robot, and this chapter showed two ways to build a drivetrain: (1) tank drive with side-by-side motors each powering a wheel or (2) rear-wheel drive with one motor for spinning wheels and a second motor for steering. An exercise worked with tank drive, and the chapter summary project worked with rear-wheel drive.

CHAPTER 7

The Motion Sensor

The Robot Inventor comes with several sensors that connect to the Hub, as well as a built-in one: the Motion Sensor, which is found inside the Hub's enclosure. This chapter will explore the capability of the Motion Sensor for tilt angle, orientation, gyro rate, and acceleration. A feature of the Hub will be described for triggering sound, with control of sound through motion data. The chapter summary project combines sensor data with motor action into a machine that always points up, regardless of the tilt angle.

Tilt Angle: Yaw, Pitch, and Roll

As was touched on briefly in Chapter 1, data can be accessed from the Motion Sensor from the Robot Inventor app. With the Hub connected to the app, going to the Hub Dashboard screen will show three motion measurements at the top of the screen as shown in Figure 7-1. These three measurements are of *yaw*, *pitch*, and *roll*.

© Grady Koch 2023
G. Koch, *Learn Engineering with LEGO*, Maker Innovations Series,
https://doi.org/10.1007/978-1-4842-9280-8_7

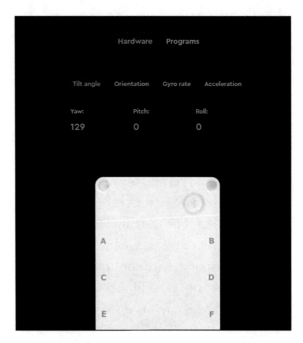

Figure 7-1. *Hub Dashboard view of the tilt angle of yaw, pitch, and roll*

Yaw, pitch, and roll are angles at which the Hub is tilted with respect to three axes, diagrammed in Figure 7-2. To develop a mental picture of these tilt angles, the Hub can be placed on a table with the front panel facing upward. Spinning the Hub while keeping it flat on the table, as in Figure 7-3a, changes the yaw. Lifting up one end of the Hub along its long axis, as in Figure 7-3b, changes the pitch. Lifting it instead along the short axis, like in Figure 7-3c, changes the roll. Each of the three angles can either be positive or negative; the angles drawn in Figure 7-2 indicate positive rotations. When controlling a robot or vehicle, the signs of these angle measurements can indicate at a glance the direction in which it might be headed.

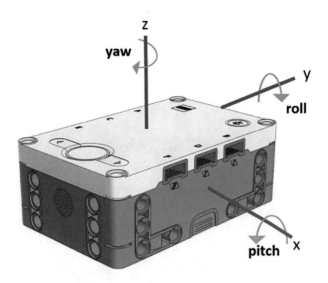

Figure 7-2. *The coordinate system for the Hub refers to three axes (x, y, and z) and the rotations about these axes as pitch, roll, and yaw*

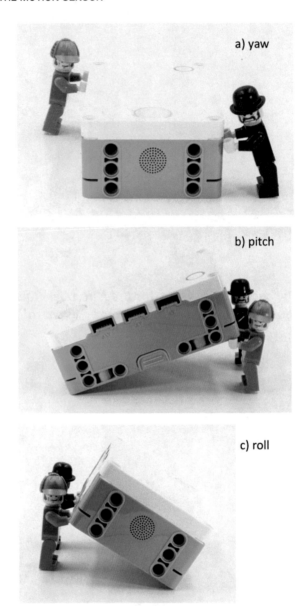

Figure 7-3. *Possible rotations include (a) yaw, (b) pitch, and (c) roll*

An important feature in tilt angles is to what an angle is based on. In other words, what orientation the Hub is in if the roll, pitch, and yaw are all zero? Roll and pitch have a zero that's easy to understand in that when the Hub is resting on a table with the control panel facing up, then the roll and pitch are zero. Yaw is a little more complicated in that the desired orientation of zero may depend on the application. For example, zero yaw may be desired to point north so that directions can be correlated with compass heading. Or, if building a robot that travels across a table top, zero yaw may be desired to align with a side of the table.

Because of these requirements, the Robot Inventor allows setting zero yaw. This is done by placing the Hub on a stable surface (such as a table) and pointing the Hub in the direction desired for zero, then going to the Hub's front panel to power it off by pressing the center button. After powering the Hub back up, without moving it, the Hub's yaw will now indicate zero. All movement in yaw will now be referenced to this zero. Yaw can also be zeroed in a program with a Word Block or Python function.

Exercise: Programming with Tilt Data

Tilt data from the Motion Sensor allows the Hub to easily be turned into an alarm system. This alarm will set off an alert on the Hub's speaker if the measured roll or pitch exceeds 5 degrees. This alarm could be placed on or inside some object that needs to be protected from someone walking away with. Or the alarm can be turned into a game to challenge someone to pick up the Hub without tilting it or walk while holding the alarm. In robotics applications, tilt measurements are an important tool for sensing whether a robot is headed in the desired direction, carrying something, driving up or down an incline, spinning around, or falling over. There's nothing mechanical to build for this alarm, since the Motion Sensor is already built into the Hub.

Measuring Tilt Angles in Word Blocks

Figure 7-4 shows the Word Blocks code for the tilt alarm. A loop in the program continuously checks whether a button has been pressed on the Hub that would end the program. Inside the loop is a conditional that checks the Hub's roll and pitch angles. Noteworthy blocks are described following Figure 7-4.

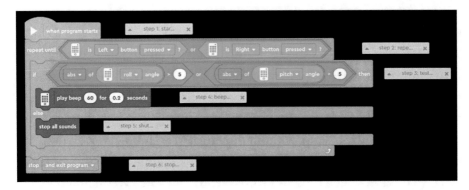

Figure 7-4. *Word Blocks code for the tilt alarm*

- Step 2: The repeat until block sets up a loop that repeats indefinitely until the condition is met of pressing a button on the Hub. This button press provides a way of exiting the program.

- Step 3: The if then else block tests the value of the roll and pitch angles measured by the Hub in its if part. If either angle is greater than 5 degrees, the then part of the block is run. If the condition isn't met, the else part runs instead. These angles could either be positive or negative, which doesn't matter for this application, so the absolute value operator is used to disregard the positive or negative signs.

- Step 4: The play beep block makes a sound on the Hub's speaker to sound an alarm. This block is within the *then* section of the conditional setup in step 3.

- Step 5: The stop all sounds block shuts off the speaker, since the alarm condition is no longer present. Being located in the *else* section of the conditional setup in step 2, the beeping sound is shut off since the measured roll and pitch angles are both less than 5 degrees.

Measuring Tilt Angles in Python

Like the Dance Floor code from Chapter 2, the Python code for the tilt alarm uses a loop and *if* statement to check for a button press on the Hub to stop the program:

```python
from mindstorms import MSHub, Motor, ...
from mindstorms.control import wait_for_seconds, ...
from mindstorms.operator import greater_than, ...
import math
import hub
from sys import exit

# Create your objects here.
myhub = MSHub()

# Program "tilt_alarm".  Beep speaker if roll or pitch > 5 deg.
while True:
        if myhub.left_button.is_pressed() or myhub.right_
        button.is_pressed():
            exit()
    1 roll = myhub.motion_sensor.get_roll_angle()
    2 pitch = myhub.motion_sensor.get_pitch_angle()
```

```
3 if abs(roll) > 5 or abs(pitch) > 5:
      myhub.speaker.beep(60,0.2)
4 else:
      myhub.speaker.stop()
```

The functions `motion_sensor.get_roll_angle` and `motion_sensor.get_pitch_angle` read in roll and pitch angles from the Hub. These angle measurements are given the variable names `roll` and `pitch` so they can be referenced in the next section of the code 1, 2.

Next, a conditional tests whether the roll or pitch value is greater than 5 degrees 3. Because of the `or` operator, the condition will be met if either one of the angles is greater than 5 degrees. Since only the magnitude of the angles is of interest in this application, the Python built-in `abs` function is applied to `roll` and `pitch`. If the condition is met, a beep is played on the Hub's speaker with a MIDI note 60 for a duration of 0.2 seconds. The action under `else` will shut off the Hub's speaker 4.

Exercise: The Cat Sound Generator

Orientation is a measurement of which side of the Hub is facing upward. For example, an orientation measurement of *front* means that the front panel is facing up toward the ceiling if the Hub is resting on a table. The Robot Inventor app offers a way to take a quick look at orientation measurement by going to the Hub Dashboard and selecting the Orientation tab. Six possible sides of the Hub could be facing upward: front, back, up, down, left side, and right side.

Orientation is vital information for any robot or vehicle that can roll around, fly, navigate underwater, or find itself in other situations where there can be uncertainty as to which way is up. A quick orientation measurement can be a matter of life or death when things go wrong in a submarine or airplane. In LEGO inventions, orientation data can determine which way a robot or vehicle is facing or if a robot has had a sudden change, like falling over.

An example in working with orientation data can be found with the Cat Sound Generator described as follows, which plays a different cat sound for each possible orientation of the Hub. This exercise will also introduce the capability of playing sound on a computer or smart device as controlled by the Hub. The following problem statement summarizes the functionality of the Cat Sound Generator:

> Have your computer's or smart device's speaker play a different cat sound for each of the six possible orientations of the Hub. Use the six different cat sounds in the Robot Inventor app's library of sounds. Include a shutoff capability by pressing either the left or right button on the Hub.

This problem statement can be solved with the following algorithm:

1. Start the program.

2. Create a loop that repeats unless the left or right button is pressed. If either button is pressed, skip to step 15.

3. Test to determine whether the Hub's front is upward. If yes, go to step 4. If no, skip to step 5.

4. Play the sound *Cat Meow 1*.

5. Test to determine whether the Hub's back is upward. If yes, go to step 6. If no, skip to step 7.

6. Play the sound *Cat Meow 2*.

7. Test to determine whether the Hub's top is upward. If yes, go to step 8. If no, skip to step 9.

8. Play the sound *Cat Meow 3*.

9. Test to determine whether the Hub's bottom is upward. If yes, go to step 10. If no, skip to step 11.

10. Play the sound *Cat Hiss*.

11. Test to determine whether the Hub's left side is upward. If yes, go to step 12. If no, skip to step 13.

12. Play the sound *Cat Purring*.

13. Test to determine whether the Hub's right side is upward. If yes, go to step 14. If no, return to step 2.

14. Play the sound *Cat Whining*.

15. Stop the program.

Figure 7-5 shows a flowchart implementation of the algorithm. A loop is used to continuously run a series of tests to determine what side of the Hub is facing upward.

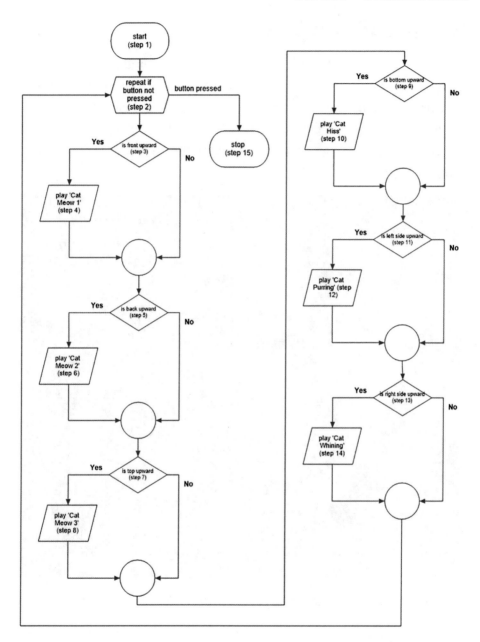

Figure 7-5. *Flowchart of the Cat Sound Generator algorithm*

The Word Blocks Code

Figure 7-6 shows the Word Blocks code for the Cat Sound Generator. In a similar technique to the tilt alarm, a loop continuously checks for a button to be pressed on the Hub that would end the program. Inside the loop is a series of conditionals to determine which side of the Hub is facing upward and play a particular cat sound. Key blocks in the program are described in detail following the figure.

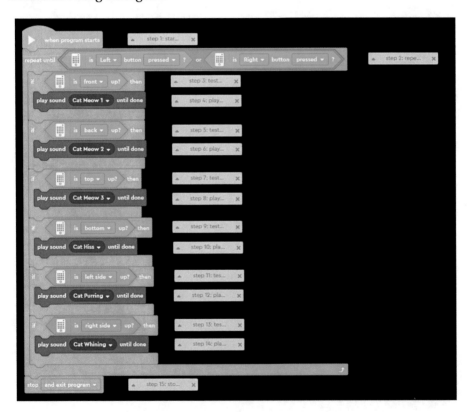

Figure 7-6. *Word Blocks code for the Cat Sound Generator*

- Step 3: The if then block sets up a condition to test if the front side of the Hub is facing upward. If yes, the blocks within the if then block will run. This if then block is repeated again in steps 5, 7, 9, 11, and 13 to test for different orientations.

- Step 4: The play sound block prompts the computer's speaker or smart device to play the selected sound. In order for the sound to work, the Hub has to be connected to the Robot Inventor app. *Cat Meow 1* is the default sound for the play sound block, and this default can be kept.

- Step 6: The play sound block triggers playing Cat Meow 2. To select this sound option, there's a pull-down menu in the oval area of the play sound block. From this pull-down menu an option for *Add Sound* will appear. Clicking *Add Sound* will bring up the *Library* tab, as shown in Figure 7-7, where many sounds can be found for selection. While this step involves selecting *Cat Meow 2*, the various cat sounds for the rest of the program can also be found in this library.

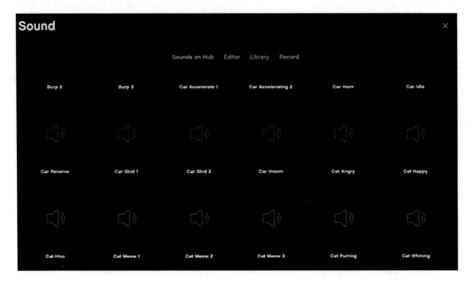

Figure 7-7. *Several cat sounds are stored in the Sound Library*

The Python Code

As in the code for the tilt alarm, the Python code for the Cat Sound Generator uses a loop and *if* statement to check for a button press on the Hub that would stop the program:

```
from mindstorms import MSHub, Motor, ...
from mindstorms.control import wait_for_seconds, ...
from mindstorms.operator import greater_than, ...
import math
import hub
from sys import exit

# Create your objects here.
myhub = MSHub()
1 app = App()
```

```
# Program "cat_sound".  Play cat sounds in App for different
orientations.
while True:
    if myhub.left_button.is_pressed() or myhub.right_button.
    is_pressed():
        exit()
  2orientation = myhub.motion_sensor.get_orientation()
    if orientation == 'front':
        app.play_sound('Cat Meow 1')
 3 elif orientation == 'back':
        app.play_sound('Cat Meow 2')
    elif orientation == 'up':
        app.play_sound('Cat Meow 3')
    elif orientation == 'down':
        app.play_sound('Cat Hiss')
    elif orientation == 'leftside':
        app.play_sound('Cat Purring')
    elif orientation == 'rightside':
        app.play_sound('Cat Whining')
```

To play sounds within the Robot Inventor app, a module is assigned as an object, called *app* 1. Rather than using an *if else* conditional, which tests for a condition and gives an alternate action if the condition is false, this program uses an *if elif* conditional. The *elif* can be thought of as an abbreviation for "else if." Essentially, it allows presentation of additional conditions if the initial condition is not met. In this case, each conditional statement asks about the value of a variable, *orientation*, that measures the orientation of the Hub 2. First, the if statement tests whether the value of orientation is 'front', and if it is, the first cat sound is played. If this first condition is not met, an elif statement then presents another test: whether the value of orientation is 'back' 3. All of the possible values for orientation are tested in this way.

Using elif is more efficient than using a series of conditionals (like in the Word Blocks version of the algorithm), because once a condition has been found to be true, the remaining options aren't tested. Word Blocks doesn't have an equivalent of *elif*. Testing for values is done with two equals signs (==) in Python. If a single equals sign were instead used, Python would assume this to be assigning a variable with a new value.

To play sounds in the Robot Inventor app, which will be played through the speakers of the computer or smart device that hosts the app, the Mindstorms function play_sound() is used. The name of the particular sound to play goes inside the parentheses as a string, such as *'Cat Meow 1'*.

Other Motion Sensor Measurements: Gyro Rate and Acceleration

Besides tilt angle and orientation, the Motion Sensor can also measure gyro rate and acceleration. Neither of these measurement functions is used much, but they're interesting to know about and study in the Robot Inventor app. As shown in Figure 7-8, gyro rate and acceleration can be selected in tabs in the Hub Dashboard screen. Both gyro rate and acceleration refer to the x, y, and z axes of the Hub, as diagrammed in Figure 7-2. In addition to seeing measurements in the Robot Inventor app, Word Blocks can pull in gyro rate and acceleration with blocks found in the *Extensions* ➤ *More Sensors* menu.

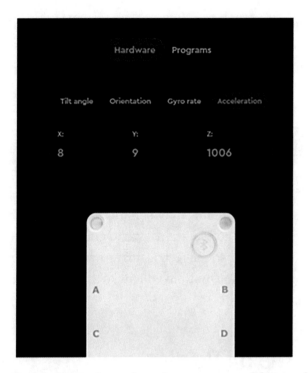

Figure 7-8. *Gyro rate and acceleration are two additional measurements that can be viewed in the Robot Inventor app*

Gyro rate is the speed at which the Hub is spinning in degrees per second, with measurements showing the rotation about each of the three x, y, and z axes. With the Hub resting on a table, the gyro rates should all be zero, since there is no motion. But picking up the Hub and rotating it, though, will make the gyro rates change. The gyro rates are measured in degrees per second. An interesting challenge is to see how high a gyro rate can be achieved by rotating the Hub by hand.

Acceleration is a measurement of how fast speed is changing, which, like for gyro rate, is measured with respect to three axes. The units of acceleration shown by the Motion Sensor are in milli-g per second. *g* is an abbreviation for the acceleration due to gravity. 1 g of acceleration is

9.8 meters-per-second-per-second, which can be a lot of words to say, so hence it's often abbreviated to g. The Hub's Motion Sensor is quite sensitive to acceleration, measuring it in units of 1/1000 of a g, often abbreviated as mg (for milli-g). When the Hub is resting on a table with the front panel facing up, it should show that the x and y accelerations are near 0 mg, but the z axis acceleration is about 1000 mg. 1000 mg is equivalent to 1 g, so the Hub is being accelerated by 1 g in the z direction. But the Hub isn't moving, so why is the acceleration 1 g? This is because the Hub would be moving with an acceleration of 1 g if the table weren't blocking the way. In other words, gravity is pulling down on the Hub, but the table is pushing upward on the Hub. The accelerations due to gravity and the table are canceling each other out, so the Hub is not moving. Setting the Hub onto its left side/right side or top/bottom will make the 1 g of acceleration move to another axis.

Project: The Up Pointer

The exercises built so far in this chapter have involved only the Hub, since the Motion Sensor is embedded in the Hub. But, of course, the Motion Sensor can be combined with external devices that plug into the Hub. As an example, Figure 7-9 shows a project called the Up Pointer, which combines the Motion Sensor with a motor. The Up Pointer always keeps a liftarm pointed toward the ceiling, no matter how the Hub is oriented in roll angle. The Hub can be rolled to any angle, but the liftarm will always point upward.

Figure 7-9. *The Up Pointer keeps a liftarm pointed at the ceiling, regardless of the Hub's roll angle*

Building the Up Pointer

A motor attached to the side of the Hub keeps the liftarm pointed toward the ceiling by using the motor's servo capabilities to rotate it to a precise angle. As the Hub is held and rolled to different angles, the motor will compensate for the roll angle to keep the liftarm pointed upward. Since the right side of the Hub is obstructed by the motor, a pair of connectors on the right side of the Hub allows sitting the Up Pointer for when its left side faces upward. When installing the motor in step 6, it's important to have the motor in its zero position as discussed in Chapter 6 (as pictured in Figure 6-1).

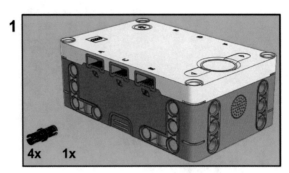

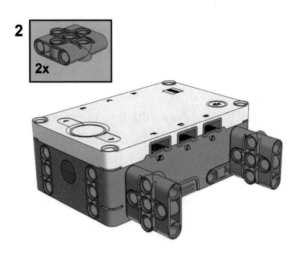

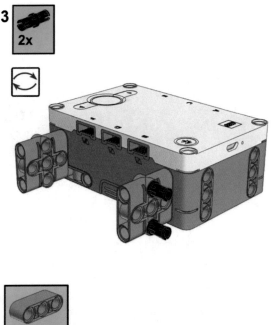

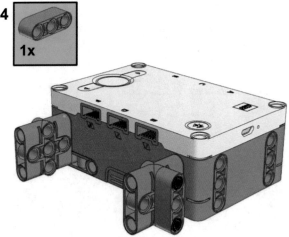

5

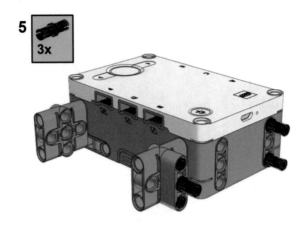

6

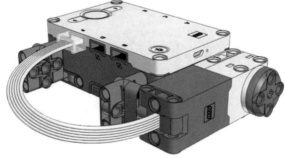

7

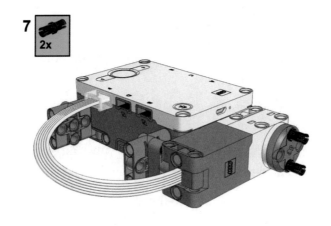

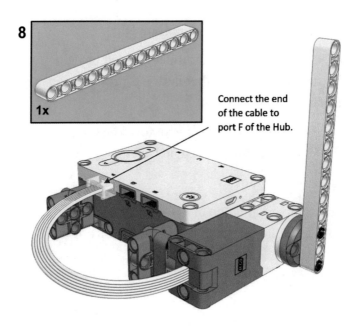

8

Connect the end
of the cable to
port F of the Hub.

Programming the Up Pointer

To program the Up Pointer, the following problem statement describes what it should do:

> Keep the straight liftarm of the Up Pointer in the upward direction, regardless of the roll angle of the Hub. Include a shutoff capability by pressing either the left or right button on the Hub.

This problem can be solved with the algorithm:

1. Start the program.

2. Set motor speed for maximum speed.

3. Create a loop that repeats unless the left or right button is pressed. If either button is pressed, skip to step 5.

4. Set the angle position of the motor to be the same as the Hub's measured roll angle.

5. Stop the program.

A flowchart implementation of the algorithm is shown in Figure 7-10, using a loop to continuously monitor the Hub's roll angle.

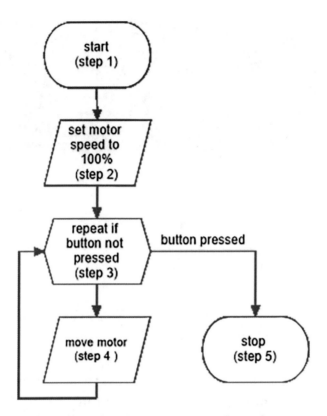

Figure 7-10. *Flowchart for the Up Pointer algorithm*

The Word Blocks Code

Figure 7-11 shows the Word Blocks code for the Up Pointer. As in all the exercises of this chapter, a loop in the program continuously checks whether a button has been pressed on the Hub so that the program can be gracefully stopped. Inside the loop, the angle position of the motor is changed as the Hub's roll angle changes. Particular blocks to note are described following Figure 7-11.

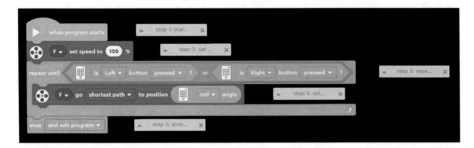

Figure 7-11. *Word Blocks code for the Up Pointer algorithm*

- Step 2: The set speed block assigns a value for the speed of rotation for the motor. Without this block, the motor will assume a default speed of 75 percent. The higher speed setting of 100 percent allows the Up Pointer to react quickly to changes in the Hub's roll angle.

- Step 4: The go to position block tells the motor to go to the angle position that matches the angle measured by the Hub's Motion Sensor for the roll angle. To read in roll angles, a Motion Sensor block (found under the **Sensors** menu) goes into the oval-shaped angle parameter.

The Python Code

The Python code for the Up Pointer is listed as follows. As described in Chapter 6 for working with motors, an object is created to use motor functions. A loop constantly checks for changes in the roll value as well as monitors for a button press.

```
from mindstorms import MSHub, Motor, ...
from mindstorms.control import wait_for_seconds, ...
from mindstorms.operator import greater_than, ...
```

```
import math
import hub
from sys import exit

# Create your objects here.
myhub = MSHub()
motor = Motor('F')

# Program "tilt_alarm".  Beep speaker if roll or pitch > 5 deg.
while True:
    if myhub.left_button.is_pressed() or myhub.right_button.
    is_pressed():
        exit()
  1 roll = myhub.motion_sensor.get_roll_angle()
  2 roll = (roll + 360) % 360
    motor.run_to_position(roll,'shortest path', 100)
```

The Hub's roll angle is measured with the same function 1 used in the tilt alarm exercise. Here, though, there's a subtle difference involving the way angles are described. Angles around a circle can be described in two ways: as ranging from 0 to 359 degrees or as ranging from –180 to 180 degrees. The Motion Sensor returns a measurement in the –180 to 180 format, but the motor function used in this Python program requires an angle in the 0–359 range. The measurement can be converted from one format to the other with a *modulus* operation, which calculates the remainder after dividing two numbers. The modulus operation is written as a percent (%) symbol in Python 2.

The final line of code spins the motor to keep the Up Pointer's liftarm pointed toward the ceiling. This function controls the motor's angle position setting, as described in detail in Chapter 6. In this case, the motor's angle is set to correspond to the measured roll angle, so the motor compensates for the motion as the roll angle changes.

Summary

This chapter showed how to work with the Motion Sensor, a sensor embedded in the Hub. The Motion Sensor can measure parameters including tilt angle (roll, pitch, and yaw), orientation, gyro rate, and acceleration. Motion data is in reference to three x, y, and z axes of the Hub, with pitch about axis x, roll about axis y, and yaw about axis z. Exercises with motion data included viewing data in the Robot Inventor app, a tilt alarm, and a sound effect generator. This sound effect generator also demonstrated how to trigger sounds using the Hub, which play on the computer or smart device that runs the Robot Inventor app. The chapter summary project combined a motor with Motion Sensor data for a machine that points the way up, regardless of the roll angle of the Hub.

CHAPTER 8

The Distance Sensor

The Distance Sensor, shown in Figure 8-1, measures the distance to an object in front of it. It can, for example, tell a robot that it may be about to run into something. Alternatively, it can trigger some action when an object gets close. This chapter will describe how to work with these distance sensing functions, first with a new type of tape measure. Then the chapter project will build a cannon that scans an area to monitor for a target to shoot at.

Figure 8-1. *The Distance Sensor*

Exercise: The Ultrasonic Tape Measure

The Distance Sensor can detect objects that are between 4 and 200 cm (2–78 inches) away. It emits a pulse of ultrasonic sound and listens for an echo from an object, then calculates the distance based on the time delay

© Grady Koch 2023
G. Koch, *Learn Engineering with LEGO*, Maker Innovations Series,
https://doi.org/10.1007/978-1-4842-9280-8_8

between the pulse and the echo. *Ultrasonic* means that the sound occurs at a pitch that humans can't hear. Some animals, including dogs and cats, can hear ultrasonic sound and might react to hearing the Distance Sensor.

The Distance Sensor (Figure 8-1) has two circular openings on the front. One circle produces the ultrasonic sound, while the other listens for an echo. As an extra feature, the circles on the front of the Distance Sensor have lights around them. These lights can add decoration or signals to inventions.

The Ultrasonic Tape Measure, pictured in Figure 8-2, serves as a good way to learn to use the Distance Sensor. This device can be pointed at an object to find its distance with a button press. Measurement results are displayed on the Hub's front panel.

Figure 8-2. *The Ultrasonic Tape Measure features the Distance Sensor attached to the Hub*

Building the Ultrasonic Tape Measure

The Ultrasonic Tape Measure is similar to the Distance Spinner built in Chapter 1, but without a motor. Building instructions are as follows:

1

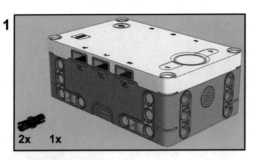

2x   1x

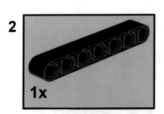

2

1x

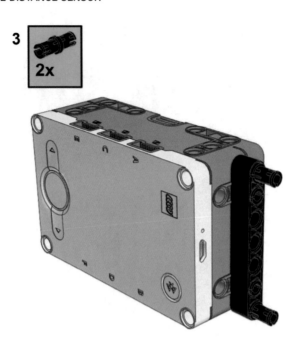

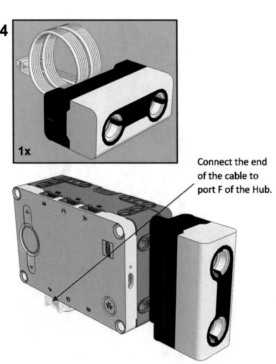

Connect the end
of the cable to
port F of the Hub.

After turning on the Hub and connecting to the Robot Inventor app, measurements can be found on the Hub status screen, as in Figure 8-3. The distance measurement should change as a hand is moved back and forth in front of the Distance Sensor. This view in the Hub status screen is a good way to check that the Distance Sensor is working OK.

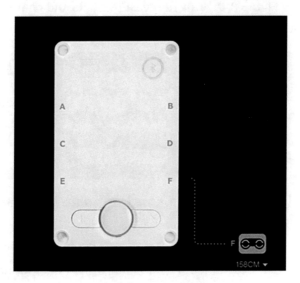

Figure 8-3. *The Hub status screen will show a measurement when the Distance Sensor is connected*

Programming the Ultrasonic Tape Measure

The program for the Ultrasonic Tape Measure takes a distance measurement and displays the result as scrolling text on the Hub's front panel. Also, the lights that surround the circles on the face of the sensor will be activated as an indication that a measurement is being made. This light feature doesn't affect the sensor's primary function, but gives feedback that the program is working. After the measurement is displayed, the program ends. Pressing the center button again will give a quick update to the distance reading.

The Word Blocks Code

Figure 8-4 shows the completed program in Word Blocks. The Distance Sensor appears in several Word Blocks, which can be identified by the icon that looks like the front of the Distance Sensor. These blocks, described in detail following Figure 8-4, bring in measurements and control the lights on the front of the sensor.

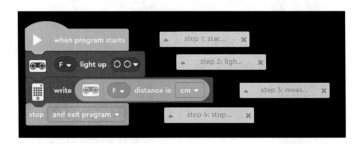

Figure 8-4. *Word Blocks code for the Ultrasonic Tape Measure*

- Step 2: The light up block turns on the lights on the front of the Distance Sensor. There are menu options to light either the bottom or top half of each circle (or both). In this example, both halves of both circles are selected.

- Step 3: The write block displays a distance measurement as scrolling text on the Hub's LED matrix. This is accomplished by using a Distance Sensor block as input to the write block.

The Python Code

The following Python code is the equivalent of the Word Blocks program. As usual, the program begins by importing modules and creating objects:

```
from mindstorms import MSHub, Motor, ...
from mindstorms.control import wait_for_seconds, ...
from mindstorms.operator import greater_than, ...
import math
import hub
from sys import exit

# Create your objects here.
myhub = MSHub()
1 demo = DistanceSensor('F')

# Program "ultrasonic_tape". Display distance  measurement.
2   demo.light_up_all()
3   measurement = demo.get_distance_cm()
4 myhub.light_matrix.write(measurement)
exit()
```

An object is created to represent the Distance Sensor and given the variable name *demo* 1. Functions on the *demo* object can now be used to control the sensor. One such function, `light_up_all()`, turns on the lights on the sensor 2. Another function, `get_distance_cm()`, takes a distance reading from the sensor. The output of this function is assigned to a variable named *measurement* 3. Results are displayed as scrolling text on the Hub's LED matrix with the function `light_matrix.write(measurement)` 4.

Project: The Scanning Cannon

Distance measurements can be useful for detecting when an object is nearby. As an example, Figure 8-5 presents the Scanning Cannon. The Scanning Cannon sweeps a coaligned Distance Sensor and dart shooter from side to side. When a target comes into view at a certain distance away, the cannon shoots to hit the target.

Figure 8-5. *The Scanning Cannon fires a dart at an object if it comes within a certain distance*

Building the Scanning Cannon

The Scanning Cannon is an extension of the Mechanized Cannon built in Chapter 5. The upgrades included now are a motor to scan the cannon in an arc, so that a target can be searched for. Also, the Distance Sensor is added to monitor for a possible target as an object that comes within a certain distance. Once a target is found, the cannon shoots a dart at it. Building the Scanning Cannon starts with the directions for the Mechanized Cannon of Chapter 5, and the following instructions start from the last step of the Mechanized Cannon. The first step, pictured as follows, is actually the removal of a piece from Chapter 5 to replace manual aiming with a motor to automatically scan the cannon.

1

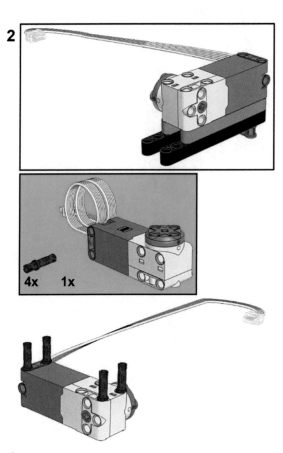

Remove the connectors and 3L axle to have a plain end on the long axle.

2

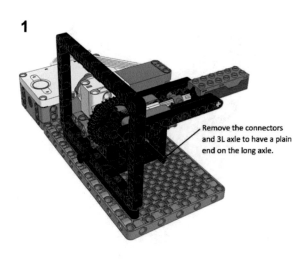

4x   1x

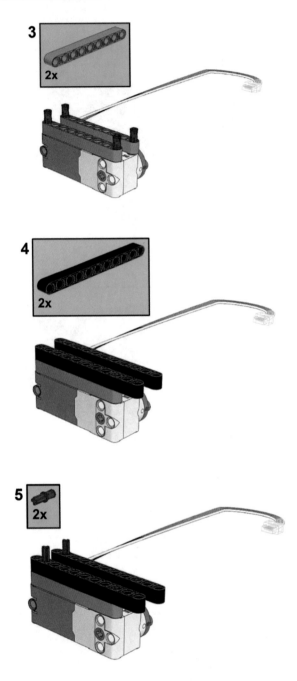

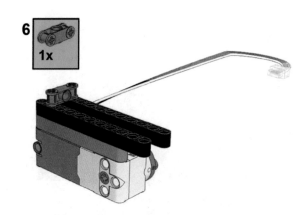

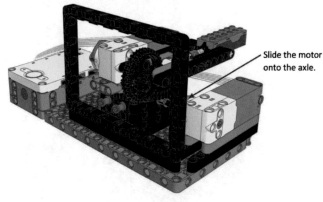

Slide the motor onto the axle.

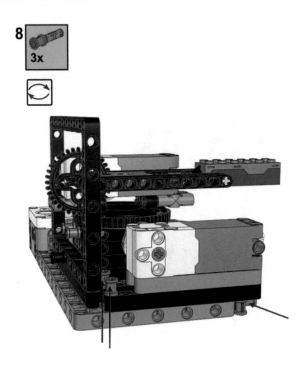

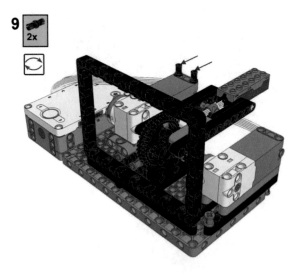

10 1x

11 2x

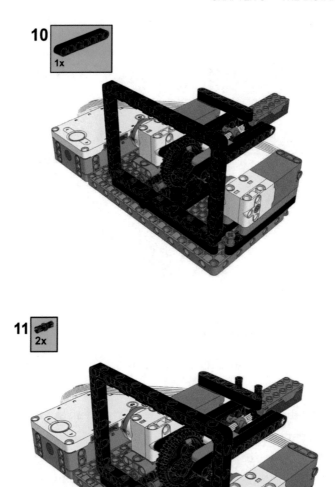

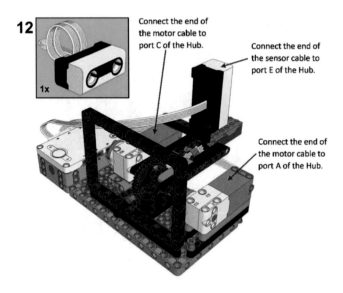

Connect the end of the motor cable to port C of the Hub.

Connect the end of the sensor cable to port E of the Hub.

Connect the end of the motor cable to port A of the Hub.

Programming the Scanning Cannon

The following problem statement summarizes the functionality of the Scanning Cannon:

> Scan the cannon so that it views through an angle of 30 degrees to either side of looking straight ahead. The time to scan through the total 60-degree angle should be three to five seconds. During a scan, light up the lights on the Distance Sensor as an indicator that the scan is active. If a target is detected during the scan that is less than 20 cm away, shoot the cannon. End the scan after the cannon is shot.

The problem statement says to scan to an angle of 30 degrees of either side of looking straight ahead, so before programming the Scanning Cannon, the dart shooter has to be mechanically set to look straight ahead. From this reference position, the scan can then be set to go 30 degrees to either side of the straight-ahead orientation. To set the straight-ahead alignment, which should look like the arrangement in building step 12 earlier, it has to be kept in mind that there is a motor and gear pair involved in pointing the dart shooter. The motor mounted off to the side of the cannon does the scanning in this design, with an axle that spins a 12-tooth gear. This gear is in turn meshed with a turntable that also acts as a gear. If the motor is in its zero home position (as described in Chapter 6), and step 12 of assembly was made with the dart shooter pointed straight ahead, then the correct orientation is done. But perhaps the motor was not zeroed before installation, or a glitch may have come up when running the Scanning Cannon, such that the motor loses its zero reference. To reestablish the straight-ahead alignment, the 12-tooth gear should be pulled away from meshing with the teeth of the turntable. With the gear unmeshed, the motor can be zeroed by spinning the rotating part of the motor by hand until it's in the correct position (with the dot lined up with the circle as shown in Figure 6-1). Continuing on with the gear still unmeshed, the dart shooter should be pivoted to the position shown in step 12 of the building instructions. Pressing the 12-tooth gear firmly against the teeth of the turntable locks in the arrangement and completes the procedure.

The next task is to figure out how far the motor has to rotate to turn the cannon 30 degrees. There are a pair of gears connected to the motor: a 12-tooth driver gear and a 60-tooth follower gear. As described in Chapter 4, this gear pair has a gear ratio of 60/12, or 5. This means that the angle that the cannon travels is one-fifth of the angle traveled by the motor. To move the cannon by 30 degrees, the motor has to turn 30 × 5, or 150 degrees. This 150-degree angle will show up in the code.

There are two ways to program the Scanning Cannon, because Word Blocks and Python offer different built-in capabilities. Word Blocks can take advantage of a capability for *parallel processing*, in which two algorithms run on the Hub at the same time. One of these two algorithms will scan the cannon, while the other will monitor for a target. The version of Python implemented for the Hub in the Robot Inventor app doesn't have a capability for parallel processing. Instead, a single algorithm using a series of sequential steps will combine the scanning and target monitoring. Because the programs take a different approach for Word Blocks and Python, the algorithm and flowcharts are different.

The Word Blocks Code

The problem statement for the Scanning Cannon can be conveniently solved in Word Blocks with parallel processing that runs two algorithms at the same time: one algorithm to scan the cannon and another algorithm to monitor for a target. The scan algorithm has the following steps. The "A" in front of the step number indicates that this program controls the motor connected to port A on the Hub:

> A1. Start the program.
>
> A2. Set motor speed to 10 percent.
>
> A3. Turn on the Distance Sensor's lights.
>
> A4. Create an infinite loop.
>
> A5. Move the scan motor clockwise to the 150-degree position.
>
> A6. Move the scan motor counterclockwise to the 210-degree position. Return to step A4.

The monitor algorithm has the following steps. The step numbers begin with a "C," as this program controls a motor connected to port C:

> C1. Start the program when an object closer than 20 cm is detected.
>
> C2. Move the cannon motor to the 180-degree position.
>
> C3. Move the cannon motor to the zero-degree position.
>
> C4. Stop the program.

Since this program runs two algorithms at the same time, the flowchart shows them operating in parallel by drawing them side by side, as pictured in Figure 8-6.

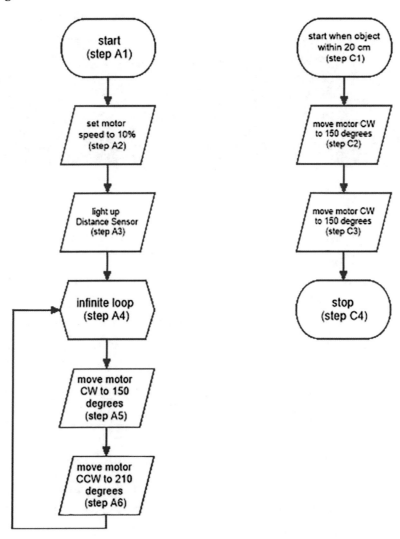

Figure 8-6. *Flowchart for the Word Blocks implementation of the Scanning Cannon*

Figure 8-7 shows the Word Blocks code, with steps A1–A6 on the left side of the screen and steps C1–C4 on the right side of the screen. This layout in Word Blocks is similar to the visual layout of the flowchart in Figure 8-6. The function of specific blocks is described following the figure.

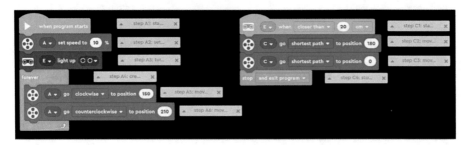

Figure 8-7. *Word Blocks code for the Scanning Cannon program*

- Step A2: The set speed to block assigns the speed setting the motor will use for the following blocks. Without this block, a motor will assume a default speed of 75 percent, which is too fast. As per the problem statement, the scan should take a few seconds to complete, so the motor speed should be set to something slow, such as 10 percent.

- Step A4: The forever block sets up a loop that infinitely repeats. Blocks inserted inside the loop will run repeatedly. The loop will eventually end when the entire program is stopped after the cannon shoots.

- Step A5: The go to position block sets the motor's angle to the position specified. As described earlier in the problem statement, the cannon should scan to 30 degrees to one side. Since there's a gear pair between the motor and turntable, the gear ratio means that the motor's angle should go to 150 degrees.

- Step A6: Another go to position block moves the cannon in the direction opposite to the prior block, making it travel counterclockwise to an angle of 210 degrees. This angle is equivalent to –150 degrees, since 360 – 150 = 210, but angles are specified in Word Blocks only as positive numbers.

- Step C1: The when block starts the second algorithm to monitor for a target that is 20 cm away or closer. There are many forms of the when block that can be found under the **Events** menu. Several of these blocks are associated with a sensor, and in this case the when block that involves the Distance Sensor is of interest.

- Step C2: The go to position block shoots the cannon by activating the cam mechanism that presses the dart shooter's button in the design discussed in Chapter 5.

- Step C3: Another go to position block resets the cannon shooting mechanism. This way, the dart shooter is made ready to reload before the next time the program is run.

- Step C4: The stop block ends the program. This action stops not only the monitor algorithm but the entire program, so the cannon also stops scanning.

The use of the Scanning Cannon for the first time involves setting it on a table with the dart shooter facing away from the operator and loading a dart into the shooter. The area in front of the Scanning Cannon should be clear of nearby objects that are closer than 20 cm to the cannon. Activating the cannon should have it scan from side to side. As the scan is off to one side, sneaking in an object from the opposite side will result in the object being shot by a dart when the scan brings the object into view.

The Python Code

The Word Blocks implementation for the Scanning Cannon takes advantage of a built-in capability for implementing parallel algorithms. Unfortunately, the version of Python in the Robot Inventor app doesn't have a similar capability. Some versions of Python offer a way to use parallel processing, but not the version used with Robot Inventor. So the following Python solution interleaves the two tasks of scanning the cannon and monitoring for a target. The program scans the cannon to a new angle, pauses to check for a target with the Distance Sensor, then moves on to a new angle to repeat the process. The algorithm for this scan-then-monitor implementation is as follows:

1. Start the program.

2. Initialize variables for parameters of scan to begin at –150 degrees, end at 150 degrees, and angular step of 25 degrees.

3. Turn on the Distance Sensor's lights.

4. Move the scan motor (connected to port A) to 0 degrees.

5. Create an infinite loop.

6. Increment the motor's angle by step, from begin to end points.

7. Move the scan motor connected to port A to a new angle position.

8. Test to determine if an object is detected at less than 20 cm distance. If yes, proceed to steps 9–12. If no, skip to step 13.

9. Move the cannon motor connected to port C to an angle position of 180 degrees.

10. Move the cannon motor to an angle position of 0 degrees.

11. Move the scan motor (connected to port A) to 0 degrees.

12. Stop the program.

13. Test to determine if the scan motor is at the end of the scan. If yes, proceed to step 14. If no, return to step 6.

14. Negate the variables for the scan: begin, end, and step. Return to step 5.

There are more steps in this algorithm than in the Word Blocks one, which shows how efficient parallel processing can be. However, this large number of steps can be easier to understand with the flowchart shown in Figure 8-8, in which there are two loops running, with one loop nested inside the other. One of these loops, at step 5, repeats the scan until a target is found at which to shoot. The second loop, beginning at step 6, steps the motor through a scan.

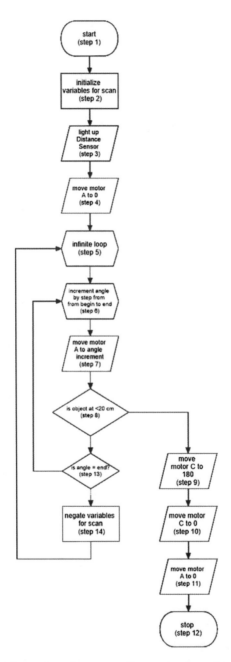

Figure 8-8. *Flowchart for the scan-then-monitor Python implementation of the Scanning Cannon*

The Python code for the scan-then-monitor implementation is listed as follows:

```python
from mindstorms import MSHub, Motor, ...
from mindstorms.control import wait_for_seconds, ...
from mindstorms.operator import greater_than, ...
import math
import hub
from sys import exit

# Create your objects here.
myhub = MSHub()
1target_detector = DistanceSensor('E')
scanner = Motor('A')
shooter = Motor('C')

# Program "scanning_cannon".  Scan for target at less
than 20 cm.
2begin = -150
end = 150
step = 25
3target_detector.light_up_all()
scanner.run_to_position(0)
while True:
  for increment in range(begin,end,step):
    angle = (increment + 360) % 360
    scanner.run_to_position(angle)
    distance = target_detector.get_distance_cm()
    if distance == None:
      distance = 200
    if distance < 20:
      shooter.run_to_position(180)
      shooter.run_to_position(0)
```

```
    scanner.run_to_position(0)
    exit()
4begin = -begin
end = -end
step = -step
```

An object is created to represent the Distance Sensor and assigned to the variable *target_detector* 1. The program then initializes variables that set the parameters of a scan 2: *begin* for the starting angle of the scan, *end* for the endpoint of the scan, and *step* for how far to move the motor's angle. The lights on the Distance Sensor are turned on as an indication that the program is working 3. Nested inside the infinite loop is a for loop, which increments the angle of the scan motor. The first time through, the for loop iterates through angles of –150 degrees to 150 degrees in 25-degree increments. When the for loop comes around for the next iteration, the motor's angles and directions are reversed, traveling between 150 degrees and –150 degrees in –25-degree increments. This reverse direction is set by negating the values of *begin*, *end*, and *step* after the for loop is completed 4. With every subsequent repetition of the *for* loop, the scan variables are negated. In this way, the scan alternates between going left and right.

Inside the for loop is a block of code that handles a requirement in Python that the angle setting for a motor be between 0 and 359 degrees. While a negative angle value may be mathematically valid, entering one into a motor control function would crash the program. Thus, any negative value has to be converted to a positive angle equivalent. As we did for the Up Pointer program in Chapter 7, a modulus operation is used to convert any negative angle values to positive values.

After the scan motor moves, the Distance Sensor measures for a possible target and assigns the result to a variable called *distance*. The function used to measure distance usually returns a number, but it will return the value of *None* if it can't find an object within the range of the

sensor. This *None* value could create a problem later in the code, so an
if statement checks if the function returned *None* and, if so, changes the
value of distance to 200. Now that the value of distance is certain to be
numerical, a check is made to see if its value is less than 20 cm. If so, the
cannon is shot and the program ends.

Summary

This chapter explored the use of the Distance Sensor. This sensor can
detect objects located 4–200 cm away and indicate distance between the
object and the sensor. An exercise used this capability to build a handheld
distance measuring tool. Then the chapter's Scanning Cannon project
demonstrated how action can be taken based on distance measurements,
in this case, to activate a motor to shoot at the detected object. While
programming the Scanning Cannon, the technique of parallel processing
was implemented to run two algorithms at the same time.

CHAPTER 9

The Color Sensor

The Robot Inventor includes a Color Sensor, pictured in Figure 9-1, that works with light. It can measure the color of objects placed in front of the sensor, as well as the brightness of light that hits the sensor. The Color Sensor includes a circular light on its front surface to provide a source of light for objects to reflect. An exercise in this chapter will work with this brightness reflection function to build a beeping tone generator. Then to use the namesake function of the Color Sensor, the chapter project builds a machine that sorts liftarms by their color.

Figure 9-1. *The Color Sensor*

© Grady Koch 2023
G. Koch, *Learn Engineering with LEGO*, Maker Innovations Series,
https://doi.org/10.1007/978-1-4842-9280-8_9

Exercise: The Brightness Beeper

The Brightness Beeper, shown in Figure 9-2, serves as an introduction to working with the Color Sensor. The Brightness Beeper will play a different sound on the Hub's speaker depending on how much light is reflected into the sensor. This light will come from the Color Sensor itself.

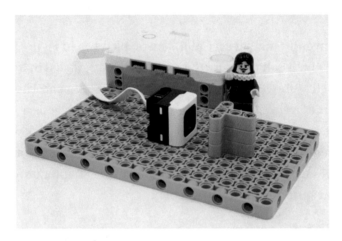

Figure 9-2. *The Brightness Beeper plays a tone that varies with brightness of light*

Building the Brightness Beeper

Building instructions for the Brightness Beeper are given as follows. One piece of the exercise is a stack of three T-shaped liftarms that aren't mounted to the baseplate. Rather, this stack of liftarms remains free to slide around in front of the Color Sensor. Its function is to act as a reflector to bounce light into the sensor.

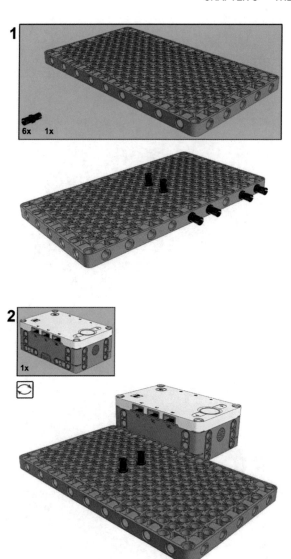

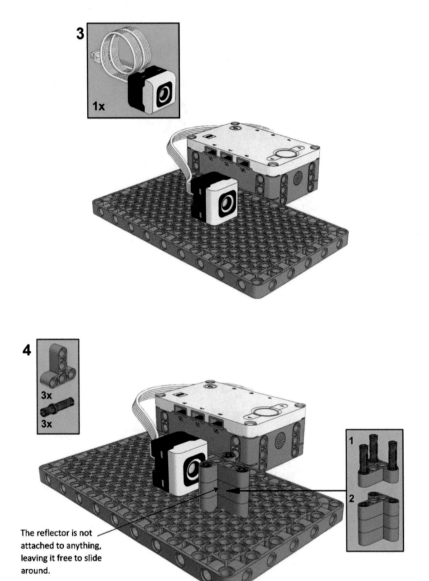

The reflector is not attached to anything, leaving it free to slide around.

A quick look at Color Sensor performance can be seen by connecting the Hub to the Robot Inventor app and opening the Hub status screen. As shown in Figure 9-3, an icon indicates the Color Sensor's state. The drop-down menu next to the icon allows selection among several modes

336

of operation. Selecting **Reflect** and then placing the stack of liftarms in front of the sensor should result in a percent value that indicates how much of the light from the sensor's built-in light source is being reflected back. Moving the reflector to various distances in front of the Color Sensor should make the light level percentage change.

Figure 9-3. *The Hub status screen will show a measurement when the Color Sensor is connected*

Programming the Brightness Beeper

While the level of light measured by the Color Sensor can be viewed in the Robot Inventor app, such as in Figure 9-3, this data can also be put to use. As an example, the light level can be made proportional to the pitch of a tone. When the light level changes, by moving the reflector liftarm stack, the pitch will change. Coding examples can be found as follows.

The Word Blocks Code

Figure 9-4 shows the Word Blocks code for the Brightness Beeper. The block that plays a sound is within a loop that can be terminated by pressing a button on the Hub's front panel. This means for ending a program has been used throughout this book. The sound-generating block is described in detail following Figure 9-4.

Figure 9-4. *Word Blocks code for the Brightness Beeper*

- Step 3: The play beep block produces a sound on the Hub's speaker. The Color Sensor's reading, represented as a percentage, is converted into the MIDI note to play. A higher MIDI value corresponds to a higher pitch, so the beep will get higher when more light is reflected into the Color Sensor. The default duration setting of 0.2 seconds is a good choice to produce a quick beep that will rapidly update as the loop restarts.

The Python Code

The following Python program performs the same task as the Word Blocks code; it plays a beep on the Hub's speaker at a pitch that varies based on the brightness detected by the Color Sensor. The program begins by importing modules and creating a *myhub* object, as done throughout this book:

```
from mindstorms import MSHub, Motor, ...
from mindstorms.control import wait_for_seconds, ...
from mindstorms.operator import greater_than, ...
import math
import hub
from sys import exit

# Create your objects here.
myhub = MSHub()
  1 color = ColorSensor('B')

# Program "brightness_beeper".  Beep speaker at pitch related
to brightness.
while True:
    if myhub.left_button.is_pressed() or myhub.right_button.
    is_pressed():
        exit()
  2 brightness = color.get_reflected_light()
  3 note = 44 + int(brightness * 0.79)
  4 myhub.speaker.beep(note,0.2)
```

An object is needed to represent the Color Sensor, given the variable name *color* in this case 1. A function associated with color is get_reflected_light(), used to measure the brightness of the light reflected from the sensor's built-in light source. The measurement result from this function is assigned to a variable named *brightness* 2. However, this *brightness* value will be between 0 and 100 percent, which won't work well to represent a musical MIDI note, as these notes range from 43 to 123. So a mathematical manipulation converts the possible brightness values to corresponding values within the desired MIDI range. This new value is assigned to a variable named *note* 3. The speaker.beep() function plays this note for a duration of 0.2 seconds 4. After the note is played, the loop runs through again to play another note.

A good start on using the Brightness Beeper is to place the stack of liftarms a couple centimeters away from the Color Sensor. A beep should result that quickly repeats. Moving the liftarm stack closer or farther away will make the beep change in pitch. But if the stack is placed very close, such that the stack almost touches the Color Sensor, the tone goes to a low pitch. This low pitch indicates that not much light is being reflected into the Color Sensor, which happens because the direction of the reflected light is not well aligned to hit the light-sensitive part of the Color Sensor.

Project: The Color Sorter

The Color Sorter, pictured in Figure 9-5, automatically sorts three-hole-long liftarms by color. Liftarms of various colors are fed into a chute at the top of the machine, and a selected color will be separated into one side of a basket. All unwanted colors go into the other side of the basket. The Robot Inventor set comes with 28 three-hole-long liftarms in colors of black, turquoise, blue, red, yellow, green, and white, so there are plenty of three-hole-long liftarms for the Color Sorter to work with. The Color Sorter incorporates many of the ideas presented in this work to combine a sensor, motors, and mechanism.

Figure 9-5. *The Color Sorter places liftarms of a selected color into one side of a basket*

Building the Color Sorter

The Color Sorter has four separate components to build: the baseplate, the chute, the pusher, and the basket. Building instructions for each of these four components are l presented as follows. The final assembly step then combines the chute, pusher, and basket onto the baseplate.

The Baseplate

The baseplate serves as a platform and connection point for all the other parts of the Color Sorter, as well as the Hub and one motor. It's important to zero the motor before its installation in step 10.

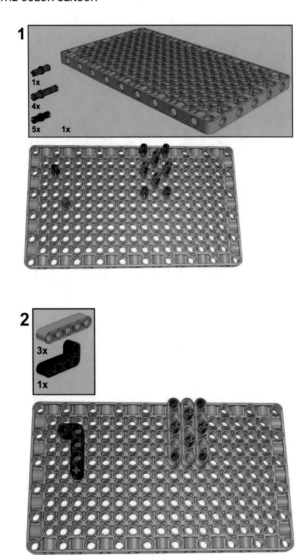

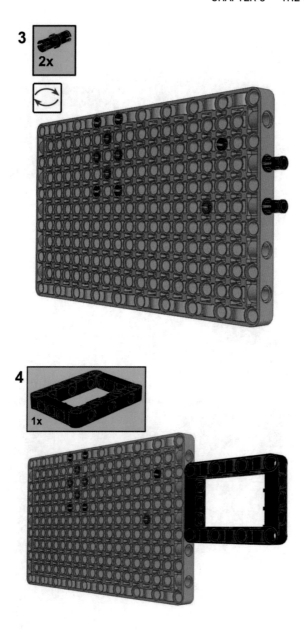

5

6

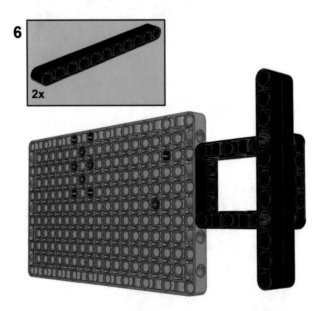

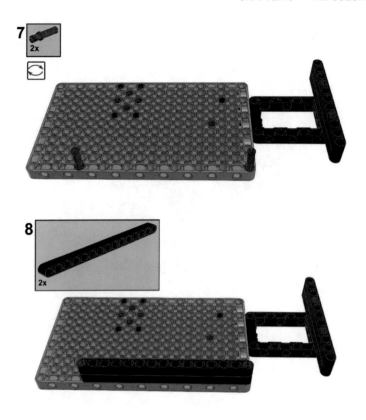

9

3x

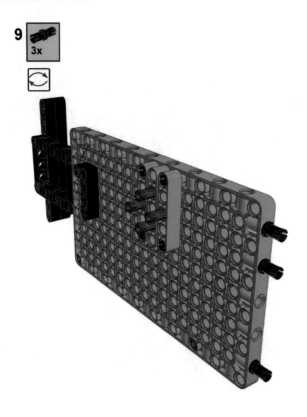

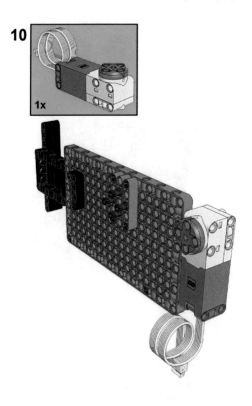

11

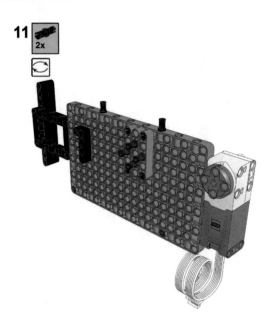

12

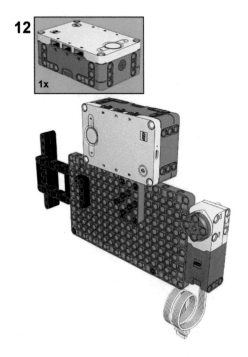

The Chute

The chute holds a vertical stack of three-hole-long liftarms to sort. As one liftarm gets pushed into the basket, gravity loads in the next liftarm from the vertical stack. The Color Sensor, also part of the chute, measures each liftarm's color. The liftarm being measured temporarily rests against the Color Sensor's face.

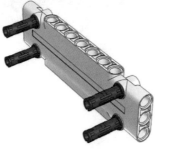

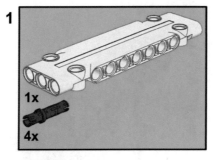

2

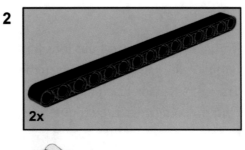

2x

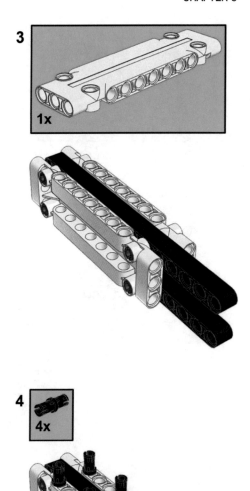

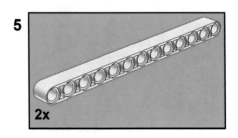

5

2x

6

2x

7

1x

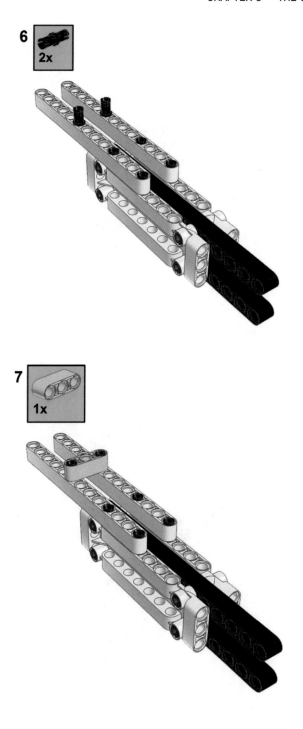

8

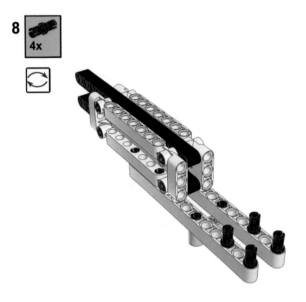

9

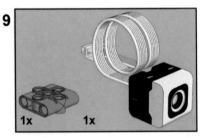

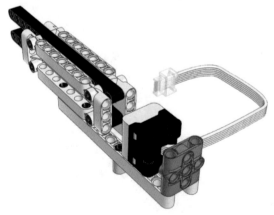

10

8x

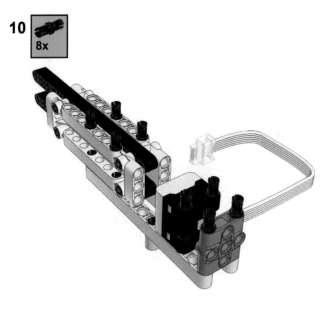

11

2x

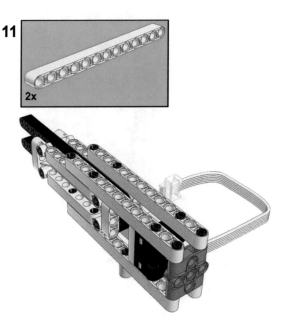

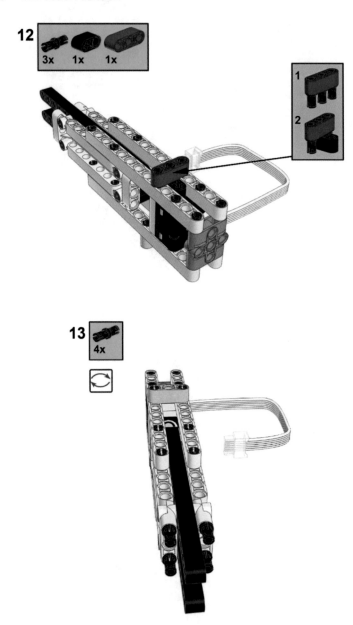

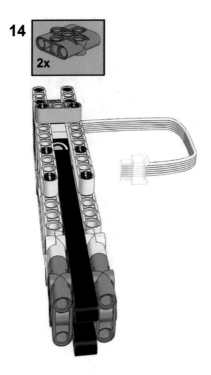

The Pusher

The pusher moves a liftarm off the Color Sensor after the liftarm's color has been measured. As the pusher retracts, the next liftarm in the chute is loaded onto the Color Sensor to repeat the measure-and-push action. The pusher is based on an eccentric mechanism, with a similar design to that built in Chapter 3. The difference here in this application is that the eccentric is driven by a motor, rather than by a manual hand crank. The motor zero position should be verified before installation in step 1.

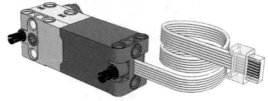

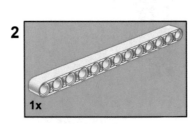

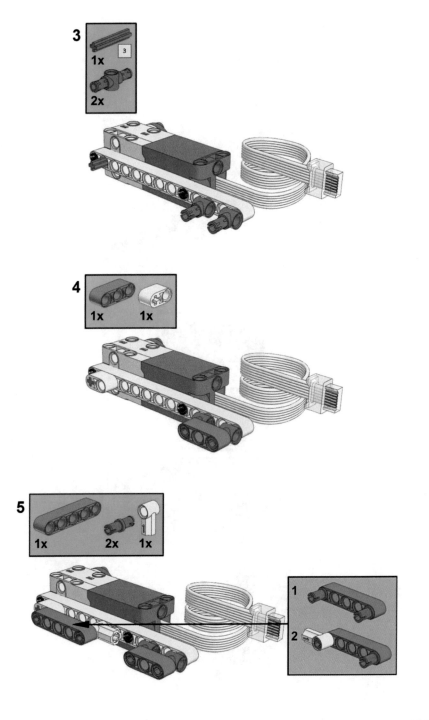

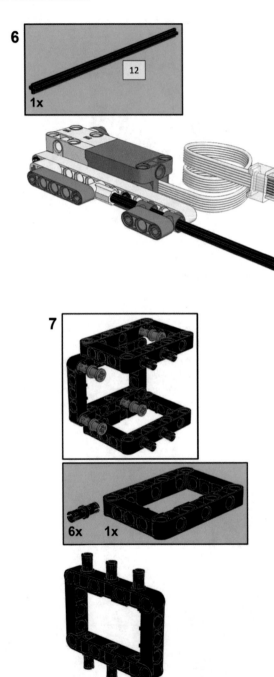

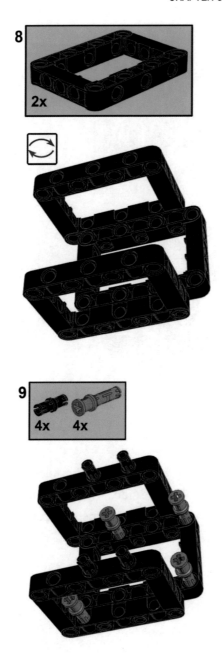

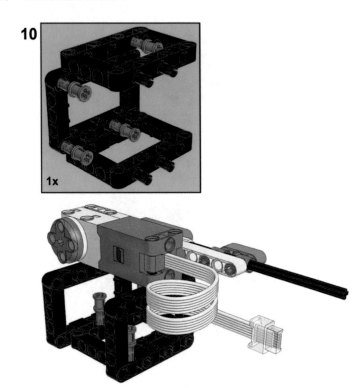

The Basket

The basket holds the sorted liftarms, with the selected color on one side and other colors on the opposite side. A motor spins the basket to change the side of the basket in which the liftarms are dropped. The two halves of the basket are separated by a wall.

1

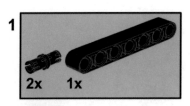

2x   1x

2

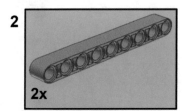

2x

3

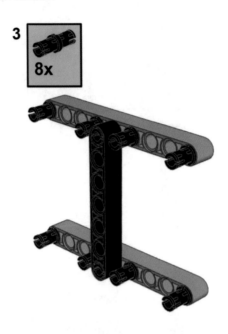

4

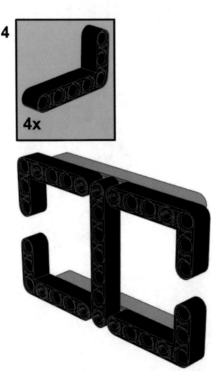

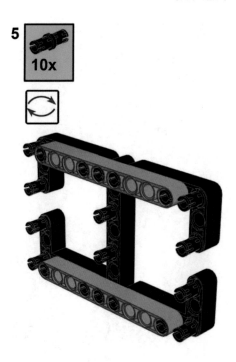

6

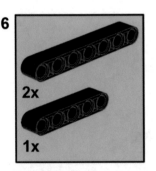

2x

1x

7

14x

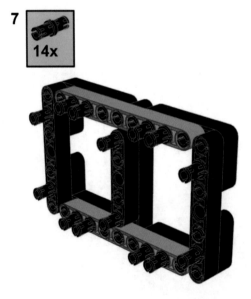

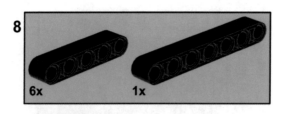

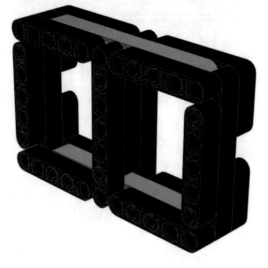

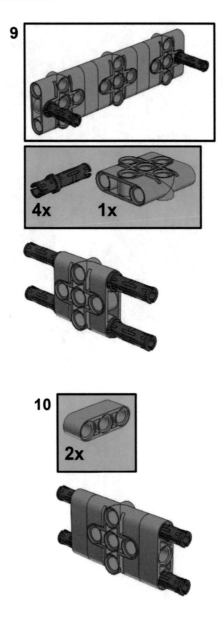

11

2x

12

2x

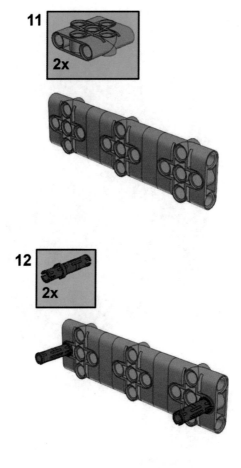

13

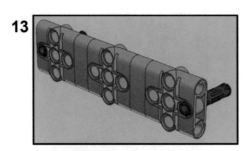

14

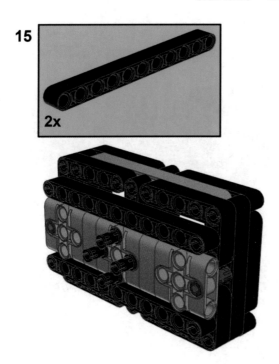

Final Assembly

The final assembly of the Color Sorter involves the attachment of the basket, chute, and pusher onto the baseplate. This placement is described in the following steps. Figure 9-6 shows a map of where the basket, chute, and pusher go, since it can be hard to see the mounting points in the building instructions.

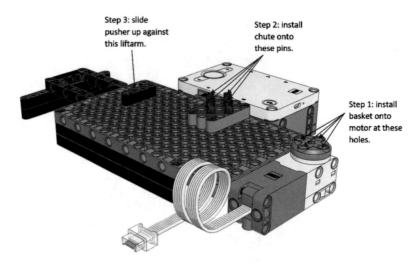

Figure 9-6. *Map of placement of the basket, chute, and pusher on the baseplate*

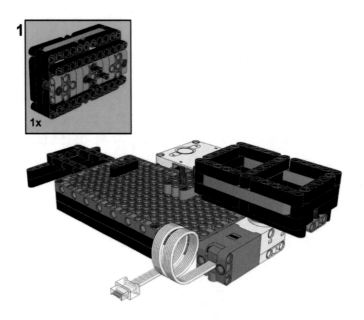

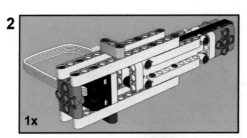

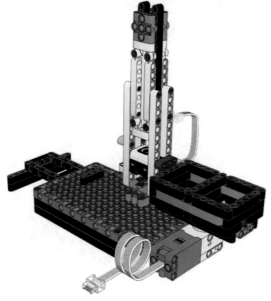

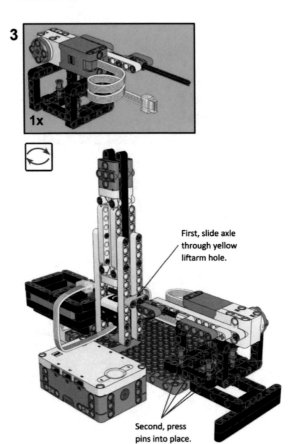

First, slide axle
through yellow
liftarm hole.

Second, press
pins into place.

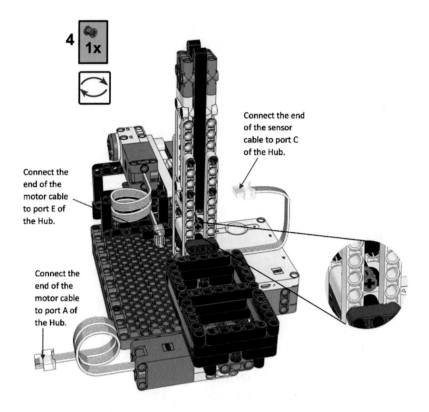

Programming the Color Sorter

The program for the Color Sorter should solve the following problem statement:

> Load a liftarm onto the Color Sensor by moving the pusher motor. Wait for one second to allow the Color Sensor to take a measurement. If the measured color is the one preselected (red in this example), set the basket motor's angle position to one side of the basket. For all other colors, orient the basket motor to the other side of the basket. Push the liftarm into the basket by moving the pusher motor. Repeat these steps for all six liftarms loaded into the chute.

The problem statement refers to several tasks involving the selection of an angle position on two motors, namely the pusher motor and basket motor. Angle settings to accomplish the required movements are referenced to a zero position, so it's critical that both motors were installed in the building steps with the motors in zero position. Chapter 6 described how to set the zero position for motors. The algorithm to solve the problem statement is as follows:

1.   Start the program.

2.   Set the basket motor speed to 25 percent.

3.   Set the pusher motor speed to 100 percent.

4.   Create a loop that repeats six times.

5.   Move the pusher motor clockwise to the 180-degree position.

6.   Delay for one second.

7.   Determine whether the liftarm color is red. If yes, go to step 8. If no, go to step 9.

8.   Move the basket motor to the 180-degree position.

9.   Move the basket motor to the zero-degree position.

10.   Move the pusher motor counterclockwise to the zero-degree position.

11.   Stop the program.

Figure 9-7 shows the algorithm in the form of a flowchart, allowing visualization of the loop that repeats six times. An if conditional is embedded in the loop to decide on the orientation of the basket.

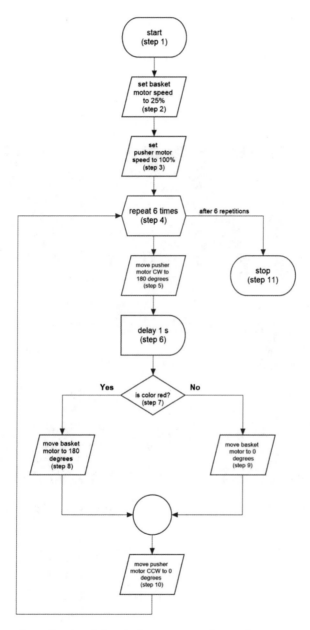

Figure 9-7. *Flowchart of the Color Sorter algorithm*

The Word Blocks Code

Figure 9-8 shows the Word Blocks code for the Color Sorter algorithm, with each code block corresponding to a block in the flowchart. Most of the program is done by an if conditional nested within a loop that repeats six times. Specific blocks to note are listed following Figure 9-8.

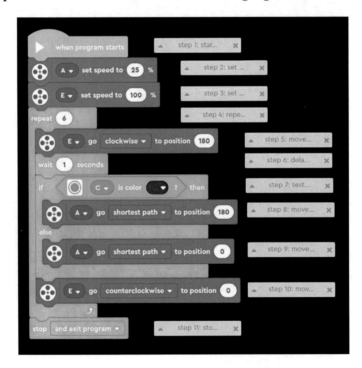

Figure 9-8. *Word Blocks code for the Color Sorter algorithm*

- Step 2: The set speed to block assigns the speed of the basket motor. Without this block, a motor will assume a default speed of 75 percent, which could cause jerky motions for the basket. A slower speed will move the basket smoothly.

- Step 3: Another `set speed to` block assigns the pusher motor's speed. Here, the maximum speed is desired to give the liftarms a firm shove into the basket.

- Step 4: The `repeat` block sets up a loop that repeats six times, then stops. Loops have been used throughout the programs of this book that run indefinitely, but this loop only runs through a specified number of repetitions. Six repetitions are used here, because the Color Sorter holds six liftarms to be sorted.

- Step 5: The `go to position` block sets the pusher motor's angle to the position specified. This motion retracts the axle connected to the eccentric so that a liftarm drops from the chute onto the Color Sensor.

- Step 7: The `if then else` block presents a condition— it checks if the liftarm seen by the Color Sensor is red. If the red condition is met, then the blocks within the first set of yellow bars will run. Otherwise, the blocks of the else section within the second yellow bars will run.

- Step 8: The `go to position` block sets the basket motor's angle to the position specified to collect liftarms that correspond to the selected color, red in this case. The basket has two halves, with one dedicated to the selected color and the other half for all other colors.

- Step 9: Another `go to position` block sets the basket motor's angle to the position specified to collect liftarms that are not the selected color. In other words, any liftarm that is not red will go into the side of the basket that corresponds to this motor position.

- Step 10: The next go to position block works with the pusher motor, as opposed to the basket motor of the prior two blocks. This action on the pusher motor shoves the liftarm into the basket.

The Python Code

The Python code for the Color Sorter is listed as follows:

```
from mindstorms import MSHub, Motor, ...
from mindstorms.control import wait_for_seconds, ...
from mindstorms.operator import greater_than, ...
import math
import hub
from sys import exit

# Create your objects here.
myhub = MSHub()
1 basket = Motor('A')
2  color = ColorSensor('C')
3  pusher = Motor('E')

# Program "color_sorter".  Sort liftarm colors into two halves
of basket.
4 for x in range(6):
   5 pusher.run_to_position(180,'clockwise',100)
    wait_for_seconds(1)
   6 measurement = color.get_color()
    if measurement == 'red':
     7  basket.run_to_position(180,'shortest path',25)
    else:
        basket.run_to_position(0,'shortest path',25)
    pusher.run_to_position(0,'counterclockwise',100)
exit()
```

There are three objects to name in the program: the basket motor given the variable name basket 1, the Color Sensor given the variable name color 2, and the pusher motor given the variable name pusher 3. Loops commonly used in this book kept running indefinitely, but here a loop is set up that only runs six times, using a for loop 4. Six repetitions are used here because the Color Sorter holds six liftarms at the beginning of the program. The sorting routine, described as follows, thus gets run six times.

A set of statements runs inside the repeated loop. These load a liftarm onto the Color Sensor, take a color measurement, and decide to which side of the basket the liftarm should go. To load a liftarm, the pusher is retracted with the run_to_position() function 5. After a pause, the Color Sensor measures the liftarm's color and assigns the result to a variable named *measurement* 6. An if conditional selects one of two options depending on the detected color. If *measurement* matches the value of red, the basket motor goes to a position of 180 degrees using the run_to_position() function 7. The second option, in the else block, occurs if the measurement isn't red. It presents the other half of the basket. After the basket has been positioned, a motor function shoves the liftarm into the basket.

Using the Color Sorter for the first time involves loading three-hole-long liftarms into the chute with the holes of the liftarm facing the operator, as pictured in Figure 9-9. If liftarms are loaded in the wrong orientation, then the liftarms will get jammed at the bottom of the chute. Six liftarms can be loaded in the chute, with the sixth liftarm sticking up a little out of the chute. Activating the program will have all the liftarms get placed into one of the two halves of the basket. Red liftarms will go in one side, and all the other colors will go into the other side. While red liftarms were used in this example case, other colors can be selected by the setting in the if then else block.

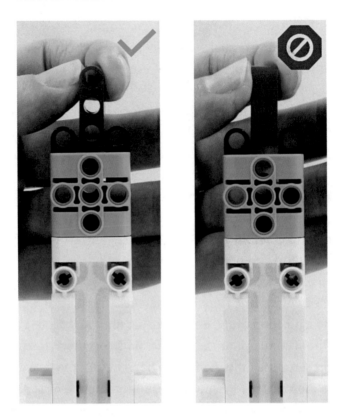

Figure 9-9. *Liftarms should have holes facing the operator for loading into the chute*

Summary

This chapter explored the use of the Color Sensor, which can measure the color of an object placed in front of the sensor. In addition to measuring color, the Color Sensor can also detect the brightness of light reflected back into the sensor from a light source built into the sensor. Color Sensor data can be viewed in the Robot Inventor app to give a quick look at measurements. An exercise built a device that beeps a tone on the Hub, with the tone changing depending on the brightness of light reflected back into the sensor. Then a more complex machine was built using color detection that sorts liftarms by their color. This project also involved motors that moved liftarms through the machine to sort them. The program for the Color Sorter involved the use of a loop that runs through a specified number of iterations, rather than running indefinitely.

Correction to: Learn Engineering with LEGO

Correction to:

Grady Koch, *Learn Engineering with LEGO*
https://doi.org/10.1007/978-1-4842-9280-8

This book was published without Series ID, Print ISSN number &
Electronic ISSN Number. This has now been updated in the book with the
Series ID - 17311, Print ISSN: 2948-2542 & Electronic ISSN: 2948-2550.

The updated version of this book can be found at
https://doi.org/10.1007/978-1-4842-9280-8

© Grady Koch 2023
G. Koch, *Learn Engineering with LEGO*, Maker Innovations Series,
https://doi.org/10.1007/978-1-4842-9280-8_10

APPENDIX A

Parts Lists

All of the parts used in this book are from the 51515 MINDSTORMS Robot Inventor set, so no additional parts need to be purchased beyond this set. But in the event that a part from this set has been lost or the reader does not have the 51515 set, the following tables summarize the parts used in each chapter's exercises and project. Part numbers are identified so that they may be found on seller sites, such as bricklink.com.

Table A-1. *Parts List for Chapter 1: The Motor Spinner*

Quantity	Item Number	Description
6	2780	Pin with Friction Ridges
1	39793	1×3×3 Pin Connector Block
1	54696c01	Medium Motor
1	67718c01	Hub

© Grady Koch 2023
G. Koch, *Learn Engineering with LEGO*, Maker Innovations Series,
https://doi.org/10.1007/978-1-4842-9280-8

Table A-2. *Parts List for Chapter 1: The Distance Spinner*

Quantity	Item Number	Description
10	2780	Pin with Friction Ridges
1	32524	1×7 Liftarm
1	37316c01	Distance Sensor
1	39793	1×3×3 Pin Connector Block
1	54696c01	Medium Motor
1	67718c01	Hub

Table A-3. *Parts List for Chapter 2: The Dance Floor*

Quantity	Item Number	Description
1	67718c01	Hub

Table A-4. *Parts List for Chapter 3: Triangular Structures*

Quantity	Item Number	Description
1	24316	Axle 3 with Stop
4	2780	Pin with Friction Ridges
1	32062	Axle 2 Notched
1	32271	3×7 Bent Liftarm
2	32316	1×5 Liftarm
1	32348	4×4 Bent Liftarm
1	32523	1×3 Liftarm
1	32524	1×7 Liftarm
2	41239	1×13 Liftarm
1	43093	Axle Pin with Friction Ridges
3	6558	Long Pin with Friction Ridges

Table A-5. *Parts List for Chapter 3: Symmetric Objects*

Quantity	Item Number	Description
4	25214	2×2 Elbow Connector
12	2780	Pin with Friction Ridges
4	32184	1×3 Cross Block
4	32523	1×3 Liftarm
2	39793	1×3×3 Pin Connector Block
2	40490	1×9 Liftarm
4	4519	Axle 3
1	48989	1×3 Cross Block with 4 Pins
2	6558	Long Pin with Friction Ridges

Table A-6. *Parts List for Chapter 3: Mechanical Linkages (The Universal Joint)*

Quantity	Item Number	Description
5	2780	Pin with Friction Ridges
2	32013	Angle Connector
2	32278	1×15 Liftarm
4	32524	1×7 Liftarm
1	32556	Long Pin without Friction Ridges
2	3708	Axle 12
2	4519	Axle 3
1	39283	Cable Clip
2	55615	3×3 Bent Pin Connector
1	59443	Axle Joiner

(continued)

Table A-6. (*continued*)

Quantity	Item Number	Description
4	60483	1×2 Liftarm
2	6558	Long Technic Pin
1	87082	Long Pin with Hole

Table A-7. *Parts List for Chapter 3: Mechanical Linkages (The Eccentric)*

Quantity	Item Number	Description
1	14720	5×3 H-shaped Liftarm
2	2780	Pin with Friction Ridges
1	31511	Circular Connector with 2 Pin Holes and 2 Axle Holes
1	32013	Angle Connector
1	32073	Axle 5
1	32271	3×7 Bent Liftarm
1	32316	1×5 Liftarm
1	32474	Ball Joint
1	32523	1×3 Liftarm
2	3673	Pin without Friction Ridges
1	3708	Axle 12
2	3713	Bush
1	3749	Axle Pin
1	41239	1×13 Liftarm
1	60483	1×2 Liftarm
1	87082	Long Pin with Hole

Table A-8. *Parts List for Chapter 4: The Many-Geared Machine*

Quantity	Item Number	Description
2	10928	8 Tooth Spur Gear
8	24316	Axle 3 with Stop
16	2780	Pin with Friction Ridges
1	32062	Axle 2 Notched
3	32269	20 Tooth Double Bevel Gear
4	32270	12 Tooth Double Bevel Gear
1	32278	1×15 Liftarm
1	32498	36 Tooth Double Bevel Gear
2	3648b	24 Tooth Spur Gear
7	3713	Bush
3	3749	Axle Pin
1	39369	19×11 Baseplate
2	39793	1×3×3 Pin Connector Block
1	41239	1×13 Liftarm
1	54696c01	Medium Motor
1	6589	12 Tooth Single Bevel Gear
1	67718c01	Hub

Table A-9. *Parts List for Chapter 4: The Torque Demonstrator*

Quantity	Item Number	Description
2	2780	Pin with Friction Ridges
1	32009	3×3.8×7 Double Bent Liftarm
2	32123b	½ Bush
1	32474	Ball Joint
1	32525	1×11 Liftarm
1	3705	Axle 4
1	3749	Axle Pin
1	54696c01	Medium Motor

Table A-10. *Parts List for Chapter 4: The Torque Demonstrator (Torque Reducer)*

Quantity	Item Number	Description
10	2780	Pin with Friction Ridges
1	32009	3×3.8×7 Double Bent Liftarm
2	32123a	½ Bush
1	32270	12 Tooth Double Bevel Gear
1	32474	Ball Joint
1	32498	36 Tooth Double Bevel Gear
2	32524	1×7 Liftarm
1	32525	1×11 Liftarm
1	3705	Axle 4
3	3713	Bush
1	3749	Axle Pin

(*continued*)

Table A-10. (*continued*)

Quantity	Item Number	Description
1	39793	1×3×3 Pin Connector Block
1	60485	Axle 9
1	54696c01	Medium Motor

Table A-11. *Parts List for Chapter 4: The Compound-Gear Spinner*

Quantity	Item Number	Description
2	10928	8 Tooth Spur Gear
1	18575	20 Tooth Double Bevel Gear
1	32009	3×3.8×7 Double Bent Liftarm
2	32073	Axle 5
3	32123a	½ Bush
1	32184	1×3 Cross Block
1	32278	1×15 Liftarm
2	32270	12 Tooth Double Bevel Gear
1	32474	Ball Joint
1	32498	36 Tooth Double Bevel Gear
1	32524	1×7 Liftarm
1	3648b	24 Tooth Spur Gear
1	3713	Bush
2	3749	Axle Pin
2	41239	1×13 Liftarm
2	4519	Axle 3
4	6558	Long Pin with Friction Ridges

Table A-12. *Parts List for Chapter 4: Two-Speed Transmission*

Quantity	Item Number	Description
2	10928	8 Tooth Spur Gear
7	2780	Pin with Friction Ridges
1	31511	Circular Connector with 2 Pin Holes and 2 Axle Holes
2	32269	20 Tooth Double Bevel Gear
2	32270	12 Tooth Double Bevel Gear
2	3648b	24 Tooth Spur Gear
2	3708	Axle 12
6	3713	Bush
4	39367c02	14×56 Wheel
1	39369	19×11 Baseplate
1	39794	11×7 Liftarm
2	55615	3×3 Bent Pin Connector
1	59443	Axle Joiner
1	60485	Axle 9
1	67718c01	Hub

Table A-13. *Parts List for Chapter 5: The Ratchet*

Quantity	Item Number	Description
1	31511	Circular Connector with 2 Pin Holes and 2 Axle Holes
1	32039	Axle Bush Connector
1	32062	Axle 2 Notched
1	32123a	½ Bush
1	32278	1×15 Liftarm
1	3648b	24 Tooth Spur Gear
1	3713	Bush
1	3749	Axle Pin
1	59443	Axle Joiner
1	6628	Tow Ball
1	70902	Rubber Band
1	87083	Axle 4 with Stop

Table A-14. *Parts List for Chapter 5: The Cam*

Quantity	Item Number	Description
1	31511	Circular Connector with 2 Pin Holes and 2 Axle Holes
1	32013	Angle Connector
1	32291	2×2 Cross Block
1	32498	36 Tooth Double Bevel Gear
1	32525	1×11 Liftarm
1	3706	Axle 6
1	3708	Axle 12
2	3713	Bush
1	40490	1×9 Liftarm
1	70902	Rubber Band
3	87082	Long Pin with Hole

Table A-15. *Parts List for Chapter 5: The Differential (Assembling the Differential)*

Quantity	Item Number	Description
1	65413	28 Tooth Double Bevel Gear
1	65414	Differential Casing
5	6589	12 Tooth Single Bevel Gear

Table A-16. *Parts List for Chapter 5: The Differential (The Differential Demonstrator)*

Quantity	Item Number	Description
20	2780	Pin with Friction Ridges
4	32054	Long Pin with Stop Bush
1	32270	12 Tooth Double Bevel Gear
2	32525	1×11 Liftarm
1	3706	Axle 6
3	3713	Bush
1	39369	19×11 Baseplate
3	39793	1×3×3 Pin Connector Block
2	44294	Axle 7
1	54696c01	Medium Motor
2	56903	8×18 Wheel
2	61254	Tire
3	64179	7×5 Liftarm
1	65414c01	Assembled Differential
4	6558	Long Pin with Friction Ridges
1	67718c01	Hub

Table A-17. *Parts List for Chapter 5: Turntables*

Quantity	Item Number	Description
1	18938	60 Tooth Turntable Top
1	18939	60 Tooth Turntable Bottom
24	2780	Technic Pin with Friction Ridges
8	32054	Long Pin with Stop Bush
1	32062	Axle 2 Notched
6	32184	1×3 Cross Block
1	32270	12 Tooth Double Bevel Gear
1	32498	36 Tooth Double Bevel Gear
2	32524	1×7 Liftarm
1	39369	19×11 Baseplate
6	39793	1×3×3 Pin Connector Block
6	4274	½ Pin
6	4519	Axle 3
2	54696c01	Medium Motor
1	60485	Axle 9
5	64179	7×5 Liftarm
12	6558	Long Pin with Friction Ridges
1	67718c01	Hub
2	99009	28 Tooth Turntable Bottom
2	99010	28 Tooth Turntable Top

Table A-18. *Parts List for Chapter 5: Mechanized Cannon*

Quantity	Item Number	Description
2	11478	0.5×5 Liftarm
1	18938	60 Tooth Turntable Top
1	18939	60 Tooth Turntable Bottom
24	2780	Technic Pin with Friction Ridges
1	31511	Circular Connector with 2 Pin Holes and 2 Axle Holes
1	32013	Angle Connector
5	32054	Long Pin with Stop Bush
1	32073	Axle 5
1	32270	12 Tooth Double Bevel Gear
1	32278	1×15 Liftarm
2	32316	1×5 Liftarm
1	32498	36 Tooth Double Bevel Gear
2	32524	1×7 Liftarm
2	32525	1×11 Liftarm
1	3706	Axle 6
1	3708	Axle 12
3	3713	Bush
1	39369	19×11 Baseplate
1	39790	15×11 Liftarm
2	39793	1×3×3 Pin Connector Block
2	43093	Axle Pin with Friction Ridges

(*continued*)

Table A-18. (*continued*)

Quantity	Item Number	Description
1	4519	Axle 3
1	49743	Dart Shooter
1	54696c01	Medium Motor
1	59443	Axle Joiner
3	64179	7×5 Liftarm
9	6558	Long Pin with Friction Ridges
1	67718c01	Hub
1	87082	Long Pin with Hole
1	99008	Axle 4 with Stop

Table A-19. *Parts List for Chapter 6: The Speed and Angle Demonstrator*

Quantity	Item Number	Description
4	2780	Pin with Friction Ridges
1	40490	1×9 Liftarm
1	54696c01	Medium Motor
1	67718c01	Hub

Table A-20. *Parts List for Chapter 6: Understanding Torque and Stall*

Quantity	Item Number	Description
8	2780	Pin with Friction Ridges
1	32278	1×15 Liftarm
1	40490	1×9 Liftarm
1	54696c01	Medium Motor
1	67718c01	Hub

Table A-21. *Parts List for Chapter 6: Powering a Vehicle with a Tank Drive*

Quantity	Item Number	Description
1	18654	Spacer
2	24316	Axle 3 with Stop
18	2780	Pin with Friction Ridges
2	32054	Long Pin with Stop Bush
1	32073	Axle 5
6	32123a	½ Bush
1	32184	1×3 Cross Block
1	3673	Pin without Friction Ridges
2	3713	Bush
2	39367c02	14×56 Wheel
2	39793	1×3×3 Pin Connector Block
2	40490	1×9 Liftarm

(*continued*)

Table A-21. (*continued*)

Quantity	Item Number	Description
2	42003	Perpendicular Connector
4	43093	Axle Pin with Friction Ridges
2	49283	Cable Clip
2	54696c01	Medium Motor
1	55889	18×14 Smooth Wheel
2	60484	3×3 T-shaped Liftarm
2	87083	Axle 4 with Stop
1	67718c01	Hub

Table A-22. *Parts List for Chapter 6: Using a Motor As a Rotation Sensor*

Quantity	Item Number	Description
14	2780	Pin with Friction Ridges
1	32498	36 Tooth Double Bevel Gear
1	39369	19×11 Baseplate
1	40490	1×9 Liftarm
1	4519	Axle 3
1	49283	Cable Clip
2	54696c01	Medium Motor
1	67718c01	Hub

Table A-23. *Parts List for Chapter 6: The Rear-Wheel Drive Car*

Quantity	Item Number	Description
2	15100	Pin with Hole
3	24316	Axle 3 with Stop
39	2780	Pin with Friction Ridges
10	32054	Long Pin with Stop Bush
2	32123a	½ Bush
2	32140	2×4 Bent Liftarm
3	32184	1×3 Cross Block
1	32270	12 Tooth Double Bevel Gear
4	32316	1×5 Liftarm
2	32524	1×7 Liftarm
2	32526	3×5 Bent Liftarm
2	3706	Axle 6
4	3713	Bush
5	3749	Axle Pin
4	39367c02	14×56 Wheel
5	39793	1×3×3 Pin Connector Block
1	39794	11×7 Liftarm
6	40490	1×9 Liftarm
4	43093	Axle Pin with Friction Ridges
1	4519	Axle 3
2	48989	1×3 Cross Block with 4 Pins

(*continued*)

Table A-23. (*continued*)

Quantity	Item Number	Description
2	49283	Cable Clip
2	54696c01	Medium Motor
1	59443	Axle Joiner
2	60483	1×2 Liftarm
2	64179	7×5 Liftarm
1	65414c01	Assembled Differential
6	6558	Long Pin with Friction Ridges
1	67718c01	Hub
2	87082	Long Pin with Hole
1	99008	Axle 4 with Stop

Table A-24. *Parts List for Chapter 7: Programming with Tilt Data*

Quantity	Item Number	Description
1	67718c01	Hub

Table A-25. *Parts List for Chapter 7: The Cat Sound Generator*

Quantity	Item Number	Description
1	67718c01	Hub

Table A-26. *Parts List for Chapter 7: The Up Pointer*

Quantity	Item Number	Description
11	2780	Pin with Friction Ridges
1	32523	1×3 Liftarm
2	39793	1×3×3 Pin Connector Block
1	41239	1×13 Liftarm
2	54696c01	Medium Motor
1	67718c01	Hub

Table A-27. *Parts List for Chapter 8: The Ultrasonic Tape Measure*

Quantity	Item Number	Description
4	2780	Pin with Friction Ridges
1	32524	1×7 Liftarm
1	37316c01	Distance Sensor
1	67718c01	Hub

Table A-28. *Parts List for Chapter 8: The Scanning Cannon*

Quantity	Item Number	Description
2	11478	0.5×5 Liftarm
1	18938	60 Tooth Turntable Top
1	18939	60 Tooth Turntable Bottom
28	2780	Pin with Friction Ridges
1	32013	Angle Connector
8	32054	Long Pin with Stop Bush
1	32073	Axle 5
1	32184	1×3 Cross Block
1	32270	12 Tooth Double Bevel Gear
1	32278	1×15 Liftarm
2	32316	1×5 Liftarm
1	32498	26 Tooth Double Bevel Gear
3	32524	1×7 Liftarm
4	32525	1×11 Liftarm
1	3706	Axle 6
1	3708	Axle 12
3	3713	Bush
1	37316c01	Distance Sensor
1	39369	19×11 Baseplate
1	39790	15×11 Liftarm
2	39793	1×3×3 Pin Connector Block
2	40490	1×9 Liftarm

(continued)

Table A-28. (*continued*)

Quantity	Item Number	Description
4	43093	Axle Pin with Friction Ridges
1	49743	Dart Shooter
2	54696c01	Medium Motor
3	64179	7×5 Liftarm
13	6558	Long Pin with Friction Ridges
1	67718c01	Hub
1	87082	Long Pin with Hole
1	99008	Axle 4 with Stop

Table A-29. *Parts List for Chapter 9: The Brightness Beeper*

Quantity	Item Number	Description
6	2780	Pin with Friction Ridges
1	37308c01	Color Sensor
1	39369	19×11 Baseplate
3	60484	3×3 T-shaped Liftarm
3	6558	Long Pin with Friction Ridges
1	67718c01	Hub

Table A-30. *Parts List for Chapter 9: The Color Sorter*

Quantity	Item Number	Description
2	15458	3×11 Panel
91	2780	Pin with Friction Ridges
1	32013	Angle Connector
4	32054	Long Pin with Stop Bush
1	32140	2×4 Bent Liftarm
4	32278	1×15 Liftarm
11	32316	1×5 Liftarm
5	32523	1×3 Liftarm
4	32524	1×7 Liftarm
4	32525	1×11 Liftarm
4	32526	3×5 Bent Liftarm
2	3673	Pin without Friction Ridges
1	3708	Axle 12
1	3713	Bush
1	37308c01	Color Sensor
1	3749	Axle Pin
1	39369	19×11 Baseplate
6	39793	1×3×3 Pin Connector Block
2	40490	1×9 Baseplate
5	41239	1×13 Liftarm
1	4519	Axle 3

(*continued*)

Table A-30. (*continued*)

Quantity	Item Number	Description
2	54696c01	Medium Motor
2	60483	1×2 Liftarm
4	64179	7×5 Liftarm
18	6558	Long Pin with Friction Ridges
1	67718c01	Hub
2	87082	Long Pin with Hole

Index

A

Acceleration, 294–296
Add comment selection, 33
Algorithm, 25
Angle, 215, 216
    position, 243
    sensor, 215
    settings, 225
    speed demonstrator, 217
    in Word Blocks, 223
Angle demonstrator, 217, 398
    Python, 224, 225
    in Word Blocks, 223–225
Angular bend, 86–92
Assembling, 168, 169, 171
Axles, 66, 67

B

Baseplate, 341–349
Basket, 362–371
    attachment, 371
    liftarms, 341
    liftarm's color, 349
    map of placement, 372
    motor's angle position, 375
    sorted liftarms, 362
    speed, 378

Beep block, 285
Beeping, 39, 55
Bent liftarms, 62, 63
Beveled gears, 102–104
Blocks, 324, 325
Bluetooth, 5, 20
Brightness Beeper, 405
    building instructions, 334–340
    built-in light source, 337
    Hub, 336
    Hub's speaker, 334
    liftarms, 337
    Python, 338–340
    Robot Inventor, 336
    Word Blocks code, 338
Bushes, 66, 67
Button press, 54

C

Cam, 394
    axle end, 163
    building elements, 163
    circular element, 167
    gear function, 163
    light lifting motion, 162
    nudging, 162
    off-center axle attachment, 166

© Grady Koch 2023
G. Koch, *Learn Engineering with LEGO*, Maker Innovations Series,
https://doi.org/10.1007/978-1-4842-9280-8